Felt It!

Felt It!

20 Fun & Fabulous Projects to Knit & Felt

Maggie Pace

Storey Publishing

The mission of Storey Publishing is to serve our customers by publishing practical information that encourages personal independence in harmony with the environment.

Edited by Alison Kolesar and Gwen Steege
Art direction and text design by Cynthia McFarland
Cover design by Kent Lew
Photography by © Nicholas Whitman
Photo styling by Robin Tesoro
Illustrations by Christine Erikson
Text production by Jennifer Jepson Smith
Indexed by Susan Olason, Indexes & Knowledge Maps

Printed in Hong Kong by Elegance
10 9 8 7 6 5 4 3 2 1

Library of Congress Cataloging-in-Publication Data

Pace, Maggie.
    Felt it : 20 fun and fabulous projects to knit and felt / Maggie Pace.
        p. cm.
    Includes bibliographical references and index.
    ISBN-13: 978-1-58017-635-4; ISBN-10: 1-58017-635-6 (pbk. : alk. paper) 1. Knitting—Patterns.
2. Felting. I. Title.

TT820.P16 2006
746.43'2041—dc22

                                                                                    2006023061

*To Joan —
my mom,
business partner,
and best friend*

Acknowledgments

First, I would like to thank my husband, Steve Pace, who did double duty on the family front so that I could knit day and night to create and test the patterns in this book. His tireless support and enthusiasm for my work is the main reason this book came to life and our kids aren't the only ones wearing my designs. He is the motor that keeps us all running, and for that I am eternally grateful. I'd like to thank our children, Kendal and Callum, for their unconditional love — and also for the use of their little heads to size my children's hats. I'd like to thank my mom, who somehow agreed with me when I said I'm going to write a knitting book and wouldn't she like to test every pattern? She has been my biggest supporter, my teacher, and my friend, from the time she taught me to knit when I was 5 to today.

I would like to thank my technical editor, Dot Ratigan, for the hours on the phone ironing out kinks and in some cases major wrinkles in the patterns. Dot, your careful eye is unparalleled. Many thanks to my editors at Storey, especially Gwen Steege, who helped to guide me through the complicated process of transforming 20 patterns into a cohesive book. Thanks to Alison Kolesar for her careful editing of the patterns and final pages.

My heartfelt thanks to Rebecca Klassen, who lent hours of knitting and problem-solving to several patterns in this book. Her design input and consistent encouragement were essential to its completion. Thanks to Kathleen Lussier-West, who was integral in the structural design of the Night Star Wrap.

Kathleen does amazing things with beads, as is evidenced on the wrap and the Star Choker.

The many knitters who tested these designs once, twice, and sometimes three times deserve a huge thank you: Joan Benson, Rebecca Klassen, Trish Egan, Jan Hanson, Joan Goldstein, Lisa Claybaugh, Claire Splan, Theresa Shoals, Mayumi Hughes, Lisa Stoeltje, Jasmine Castillo, Nita Sumrall, and Sarjan Holt.

Thanks to Kelly Wilkinson, my business partner, for her hours of work at Pick Up Sticks! that freed me to complete my manuscript. Kelly, thanks for taking this on! Without you none of this would be possible.

Thanks to my neighbor Joe (and his screwdriver) for rescuing the patterns from my failed hard drive the day of my manuscript deadline!

Thanks to my mother-in-law, Elaine Pace, whose quiet support through all of this has meant much more to me than she knows. My thanks to Gabrielle Mitchell for making me believe I had something worth pursuing. Thanks to Priss Ellingboe and Elaine Brody, who laid the groundwork for Pick Up Sticks! Thanks to Christina Stork at Article Pract in Oakland for purchasing my first pattern and helping me to believe in my designs. Thanks to Ellen Roosevelt at Stash in Berkeley for telling me I had something worth developing with my knit flowers.

I'd like to thank the many yarn companies that supplied the yarn for the patterns. Finally, I'd like to thank the retail store owners, who continue to take a chance on independent pattern designers.

contents

Take the Plunge!

Before you dive into this book, be forewarned: It could lead to a serious addiction. The first time I felted, I shrunk down an old wool hat just to see what would happen. I threw it into a pot of boiling water and beat it around with a wooden spoon. After about 20 minutes, that hat was small, stiff, and bowl shaped. I wasn't all that thrilled with the woolen bowl (though it did make a nice paper-clip holder), but I was thrilled with the process. I loved watching the fibers transform in front of my eyes.

Next thing I knew, I was felting everything in sight. I knit huge, grocery-bag-sized totes and shrunk them into dainty little purses. I knit clown hats that skimmed my chin and washed them into cute 1920s cloches with brims that I could shape as I wished. I knit complex Fair Isle flower patterns that felted into smooth, unpixelated images that really look like blossoms. I've been developing patterns ever since, and I'm more than happy to share!

What You Need to Get Started

Felting takes needles, wool, a washing machine — and a little moxie. The first three are really the only objects you need to get started with felting, and a little later, I'll help you make the right selections. But first, let's talk about the felting essential that's harder to come by: *moxie.*

I admit that felting is a bit nerve-racking. As you knit, several questions arise: Is this pattern *right?* Doesn't this purse look *disproportionate?* Will the yarn I'm using felt *correctly?* How will a hat sized for André the Giant *ever* fit my three-year-old daughter? And so on.

Because of its imprecise nature, felting requires a healthy dose of free-spiritedness, the willingness to break the rules, and the ability to throw the concept of gauge out the window. In short, felting requires guts: You need guts to slide ten hours of knitting and $30 of nonwashable yarn into steaming hot water. You need guts to knit without knowing how the measurements are going to turn out. You need guts to trust a pattern that seems like it's flat-out wrong.

The "moxie" that it takes to felt your knitting depends simply on your willingness to break knitting rules and throw the concept of gauge out the window.

Some of us come to this book with the required moxie. If that "some of us" is not you, *don't worry about it!* You are holding the "How to Gain Felting Moxie" guideline in your hands. Throughout the book, I'll point out the times you need to break the rules. I'll tell you when gauge makes not one bit of difference or when you have to pay attention to it. I'll be specific about how to felt the piece, when to pull it out of the washer, and how to shape it when it's wet.

As you knit and felt the projects in this book, you'll start to get a feel for the process. You'll understand what it means when felters say things like, "Yeah, the bag is so long because it's gonna shrink more in the length." You'll start to trust the patterns as you anticipate how the piece will shrink. You'll more confidently swap yarns as you get to know how different manufacturers' wools felt.

CHOOSING THE RIGHT MATERIALS

All felting projects begin with a 100% wool or a wool blended with another animal fiber that shrinks, such as alpaca. (Wool blends that contain a synthetic will not felt.) Be sure, too, that the wool has not been treated to be machine washable. This sounds simple enough, but wools come in many varieties and each variety felts uniquely. In standard knitting, it's enough to check your gauge, make the proper adjustments, and feel fairly confident that the finished item will size correctly. In felting, if you've chosen a yarn that doesn't felt (for instance, a bleached white), the finished piece will fail even if your gauge is spot on. This is why I often say pre-felted gauge doesn't matter; it's what happens in the washing machine that counts.

When I started researching materials for this book, I bought wool from about 15 different manufacturers and knit each one into a 4" × 4" square, using a different number of cast-on stitches as needed to make them uniform in size. Then I felted each one for the same amount of time. The swatches shown below and on pages 18–19 show how differently they felted. Not only did each swatch size differently, but their textures also varied greatly. Some were fuzzy, some were flat, and some just sort of matted up. Some wools felted quickly, and some never did felt — meaning their stitches wouldn't disappear.

Felted samples of various yarns

While this was an interesting experiment, it doesn't prove that it's impossible to predict the results of felting. You can predict your success and finished sizes. If I choose all of the wools that felt the way I like and make sure that they are all the same weight, I can cast on the same number of stitches and knit the same number of rows and make them felt to the same size. The place to make this happen is in the washing machine. Some swatches take 10 minutes, others take 5; but in the end, all of the swatches are fairly uniform. That's why felting patterns work.

THE BASICS ON HOW WOOL FELTS

If you were to look under a microscope at one of the fine fibers that makes up a strand of yarn (the "fuzz" that you see on the piece below), you'd find a scaly surface that would remind you of an insect leg. This scaly surface enables wool to felt. When the fiber is introduced to heat and moisture, the scales open up. Add agitation to the mix, and the blossomed fibers catch one another and become entangled. A chemical process occurs at this point, permanently binding the fibers together. That's why you can slice right through felt and it will not fray. If these scales are chemically altered, say through the bleaching process, the wool's felting properties change and it does not shrink as well. This definition of felting applies to all types of wool: You don't need a 100% lamb's wool to felt. Alpaca yarns and wool blends can also work as well.

Each kind of wool will felt a little differently because of the structure of its fiber and its blend. You'll know that your piece is done felting when

● it is the right size, and

● its stitch definition has disappeared.

Magnified strand of yarn

SOME FACTS ABOUT FELT

- Knitted wool felts more in length than in width.

- The more agitation, the quicker the wool felts.

- The wool shrinks more rapidly once the stitches start to disappear.

- Alpaca yarns become fuzzier than 100% wool when felted, but some alpaca yarns tend to mat. (Matting is when the fuzzy bits from the alpaca chunk together and lay flat, looking a bit like a poodle in need of grooming.) In contrast, an alpaca yarn that felts nicely has a fluffy, cashmerelike feel to it.

- Some whites and light-colored wools will never felt, depending on the yarn manufacturer. Ask your local yarn store owner before buying a white or light-colored yarn for a felting project so he or she can steer you in the right direction. (Cascade's 220 line includes a cream-colored wool that felts beautifully. I used it for the Elegant Lily [page 127].)

- Darker colors felt more quickly than lighter colors.

What does all this mean to you?

If you're new to felting, I suggest you play it safe and stick with the yarns I recommend for the patterns in this book. All of the yarns I chose are readily accessible in your local yarn stores or on the Internet. (For yarn resources, see page 148.)

STRIKING OUT ON YOUR OWN

If you're ready to venture out and want to use a yarn that's not suggested, go for it! But before you do, here are some suggestions.

Yarn weight. Choose a yarn of the same weight as the one recommended in the pattern. If the pattern calls for a 100% worsted wool or wool blend, for instance, use a worsted. When I was testing the Petals & Stems Purse (page 57), even though I knew better, I combined sport- and worsted-weight yarns. The project failed miserably. The sport yarn shrank more quickly than the worsted, and as a result, the bag turned out cattywompus!

Swatching. Swatching is important — not so much to check the gauge but to ensure that the yarn felts. Make a large swatch and run it through the washer. Evaluate it: Did the yarn mat? Is it too fuzzy? Did the stitches disappear and the material stiffen? If you are working an intarsia or Fair Isle pattern, did the colors felt at an even rate? Did the colors bleed?

When you swatch, don't obsess about the gauge. You'll just become frustrated. If the yarn is the same as the recommended weight and you like the way it felts, you'll be able to control the final measurements when you wash it and thus reach a result close to what's recommended in the pattern.

AHHH . . . DO I HAVE TO CHECK THE GAUGE?

Who likes to check gauge anyway? I don't. I just want to jump right into my project. That's why felting nonwearable items is great. If you've chosen a yarn the same weight as I recommend and you know it will felt, you can pretty much get clicking. Any problems will come out in the wash, as they say.

You should check your prefelting gauge when it comes to hats, however. If your tension is tight (that is, you tend to knit tightly), knit a hat in the larger size so you have more room to shrink the hat down to the correct size in the washing machine. If you're making the largest-sized hat and you have a tight tension, you can go up a needle size to give yourself a little wiggle room. If your tension is loose (that is, you tend to knit loosely), don't make any adjustments.

A NEEDLING ISSUE

The patterns in this book uniformly recommend US #10 (6 mm) needles even though the yarn band label often calls for needles that are US #7 (4.5 mm) or smaller. The loose tension attained by US #10 enhances the friction between the stitches as the piece is felting, making it shrink better. If the stitches are too snug against each other, felting is inhibited. A larger piece also allows a broader margin for sizing in the washing machine.

Left: Prewashed swatch
Right: Same piece after felting

My Basic Felting Technique

Legend has it that the Huns discovered felting when they used layers of wool for their saddles. The agitation, heat, and sweat generated on an all-day ride produced a felt so tightly entwined it was waterproof. You'll employ a different method for felting. It will be just as effective, but you don't need a horse — just a washing machine. It doesn't matter what kind of washing machine it is, as long as it runs hot water, has a high agitation cycle, and can be stopped in the middle of the cycle so you can check your work.

1 **Prepare the item.** Begin by preparing your item for felting. Make sure the ends are *securely* woven down. If necessary, knot the ends on the back so they don't come undone during felting, which will cause holes. If you're working with a seamed piece, make sure the seams are smooth and not puckered before felting.

2 **Set up the washing machine.** Set your machine to "hot" on a low-water, high-agitation cycle. Let the basin fill with hot water.

3 **Agitate and check.** When the agitator starts moving, add the piece. It will take a few minutes for the piece to show signs of shrinkage. Once it does, check it often, at least every 1 or 2 minutes. Don't let the piece go through the spin cycle. If the agitation cycle is done and the piece still isn't felted, manually reset your machine to go through the agitation cycle again without letting it go through the spin cycle.

4 **Remove when done.** Pull the piece out when it reaches the desired size and texture. (See Recognizing the Magic Window on page 18.)

5 **Rinse and squeeze.** Rinse by hand in cool water, and squeeze out excess water by rolling the piece in a terry-cloth towel.

6 **Shape.** Follow the shaping directions for your pattern.

Voice of Experience: Your Questions Answered

Q *When I checked my project during the washing stage, it actually seemed to be stretching instead of shrinking. Is there something wrong?*

A During the agitation stage, be prepared for the piece to get bigger before it gets smaller. When knitted wool is wet, it stretches. It will stay stretchy like that for a while before it starts to compress. Once the stitches begin disappearing, the piece will felt quickly, so don't walk away from the washing machine at this stage.

Q *Is there anything I can do to speed the felting process?*

A If something is felting slowly, add jeans to the washer to expedite the process. Avoid adding towels because some shed lint that can become embedded in the felted cloth.

Q *My I-cord didn't felt evenly — some spots are thicker than others.*

A When felting I-cords, belts, or other long-and-lean items, check them often. If they become tangled, they'll felt unevenly at the tangle points and take on a thick-and-thin appearance that's hard to fix.

Q *I lost my flowers when I tried to felt them. Any suggestions for how to avoid this next time?*

A Place tiny items, like brooches, into a laundry bag so you don't lose them under the agitator.

Q *I thought my piece was just right, but now that it's dry, I'm unhappy with it. Is it too late to fix?*

A No matter how long a piece has been dry, if you aren't satisfied with the size or texture, you can put it back in the machine and refelt it.

Q *I've noticed that other felters use detergent when they felt items. What's your advice?*

A Lots of felting patterns suggest adding a little detergent or baking soda to the water, but I've felted both with and without and don't see the benefit.

Recognizing the Magic Window

The most mysterious part of felting occurs in the washing machine, somewhere between the moment the piece begins losing its stitch definition and the dreaded instant you realize you've overfelted. I've put things in the washer for "just a minute longer" and ended up with a hat that annoyingly rides up on my head because its circumference got just a little too small. The good thing is, once you're in the Magic Window, you can pull the piece out at any time and it will work. But, if you don't time the moment exactly right, it won't be perfect. Too soon, and brims will be too long, purses will slump, and flowers will droop. Too late, and hats will ride up, purses will lose proportion, and flowers — well, flowers just look better the longer you felt them so you don't have to worry about overfelting when you're making flowers.

You know you're in the Magic Window if

● the piece is nearing the correct size;

● when you wring the fabric by hand, the stitch definition is disappearing;

● the fabric is thickening and feels firm to the touch.

When you're in the Magic Window, proceed with caution. Let the washer continue agitating, but stand right over it. Dip your hand in frequently to check things out. Different items require different criteria for doneness. Read on for some basic guidelines for specific kinds of items.

THE CHALLENGE OF HATS

Hats are the trickiest, so let's start there. It's ideal to have the wearer present when the hat is felted. If this is not possible, use an understudy or find a bowl that measures the right circumference, according to the sizes indicated in the pattern. When the felting begins to reach the Magic Window, pull the hat out, wring out the excess water, and size it to the wearer. The stitches will still be somewhat visible and the fabric will be long and drapey. Now you have a feel for the fabric — but it's not ready yet! Put the hat back in and let it run for a minute or so more. Pull it out again and notice how much it has stiffened, and how the stitches have become blurred. Don't be surprised if the hat *feels* right, but the brim is still too long. Keep on felting! Put it back in and continue this process until the circumference and the length at the brow are proportionate and the fit feels good. When the hat is ready, pull it out, rinse it, and roll it in a terry-cloth towel. Block the hat as described in the shaping section (see Getting into Shape on page 23). If you feel you've overfelted it slightly, don't worry. It can still be stretched during the blocking process.

IF THE HAT FITS, WEAR IT

If the hat seems underfelted (you can still see some of the stitch definition) but fits, pull it out of the machine. Certain yarns — especially lighter-colored ones — won't lose all of their stitch definition. It's better to have a good fit and see some of the stitching than have a hat that isn't wearable.

RIO de la PLATA
16 sts / 17 rows
= 4" sq.

ELSEBETH
LAVOLD
ANGORA
16 sts / 17 rows
= 4" sq.

MALABRIGO
COL CHINA
16 sts / 17 rows
= 4" sq.

IT'S IN THE BAG — AND THE BELT

Purses and bags are always easier to felt than hats or clothing because they don't have to be sized perfectly. When you reach the Magic Window with a purse or bag, the trick is not to get impatient and pull it out too soon. Make sure the fabric thickens and the stitches completely disappear before removing the piece. The fabric has to be stiff enough so that the final purse or bag won't slouch. Remove the excess water by rolling the piece in a towel before judging its doneness. It's hard to tell how stiff the fabric is when it's sopping wet.

Oftentimes, handles for purses and bags are I-cords. Be careful when felting I-cords. If they get tangled in the washing process, they can shrink disproportionately — damage that can be irrecoverable. The same advice holds true for belts. It's not a question of *if* a belt will tangle in the wash, but *when.* Since belts should be felted a long time to ensure they are sufficiently stiff, don't be surprised if you have to untangle the belts several times before they are done.

Oh, what a tangled web . . .
It's important to avoid tangling belts and I-cords in your washing machine. Check them often and disentangle as needed.

Checks & Spirals Backpack, page 63

TROUBLESHOOTING FELTING

PROBLEM	SOLUTION
Woven end comes undone in washing machine, creating a hole	If you catch the hole before the piece is totally felted, it's fixable. Just sew up the hole using a yarn needle and matching yarn. Even if the repair job looks ugly, throw it back in the washer. If you've caught the hole soon enough, the new stitches should disappear into the fabric.
Hat is too small due to overfelting	If the hat isn't wet, get it wet. Stretch the fabric aggressively. Find a bowl or headform that's large enough and pull the fabric over it. Don't worry about how far you stretch the material: Your goal is to break down the fibers enough so that you can reform the hat. Let the hat dry completely before removing.
Bag is disproportionate due to overfelting	Use the same process you used for an overfelted hat. The trick here is finding the right mold for the purse. I've cut and taped cardboard boxes into the right shapes to make a structure over which I can stretch the piece.
I-cord handle tangled	Lay the wet I-cord on a flat surface and finger-press it flat. Try to make the entire handle the same width to get rid of the thick-and-thin look. Put it back in the washer and felt it some more, making sure it doesn't tangle again.
Piece went through the spin cycle and has become too small and misshapen	Get it wet. Stretch and pull it until it is the shape you want. Be as aggressive in stretching as possible. Don't worry about damaging the fabric. If it's a hat or a purse, stretch it over a mold; if it's a flat item, pin it on an ironing board or other flat surface so it stays in place. Let it dry completely before moving it and it should hold its shape.
Too fuzzy	Shave it or trim it with scissors.
An older piece is looking shop-worn	Felted items can ball up over time, especially purses you use often. You can either trim or shave the surface or you can give it a bath. Throw it in the washer for a minute or two, and then reshape it by using a mold or pinning it down. The item will look like new.

FORGET ME, FORGET ME NOT!

Even though you don't have to be careful with items like flowers, don't forget about them! It's very easy to throw a flower in the wash, get started on paying the bills, and return to the washer to find it looking like mulch because it's gone through the spin cycle. I avoid this by keeping my washing machine lid open. Many machines will automatically stop after the agitation cycle if the lid is open.

PERFECT PILLOWS, SOFT SCARVES

For pillows, I use a lighter touch than I use for purses because I want the fabric to remain soft. This means I pull the pillow out toward the beginning of the Magic Window, immediately after the stitches disappear. A lightly felted fabric will always be less stiff — and who wants a stiff pillow?

The same is true for scarves. If you overfelt a scarf, it will lose its drape and softness. Not only will it be scratchy to wear, but it also won't lay as nicely. Err on the side of caution with scarves and pull them out a little earlier. If, after the scarf dries, you feel it could use more time in the wash, throw it back in.

A JEWEL OF A PATTERN

The jewelry patterns in this book begin with 100% wool fingering yarn. Such yarn is not a likely candidate for felting. When worked on tiny needles, the stitches are tightly compressed and it's hard to get the yarn to break down. Add to this the fact that the dainty pieces don't get very much agitation in the washing machine, and they simply won't felt completely. If you know this before you start, you won't get frustrated when you can still see some of the stitch definition, even after running it through the washer three times. Personally I like the texture of the jewelry with some stitch definition still showing.

FABULOUS FLOWERS

Who cares, it's a flower! You really can't overfelt the brooches and large flowers in this book. The big concern is underfelting. If you pull the flowers out too soon, the petals will be too floppy. The stiffer the flowers, the better they look.

Getting into Shape

Wet knitted wool is much like clay. New felters are often surprised at the moldable quality of the wet fabric when it comes out of the washer. You can stretch it and pull it, scrunch it and pinch it, and the material mostly holds its shape. Good shaping requires that you force the wet wool to stay in the desired position until it is completely dry. The methods I use include molding, pinning, scrunching, and compressing.

MOLDING

Anything in your house can be used as a mold. My kids' plastic bowls are perfect shapers for my infant-sized hats. Square plastic punch pitchers make excellent molds for totes. You can make a mold using strong cardboard, tape, and scissors.

You need a mold for any three-dimensional object that has a hard time holding its shape as it's drying. If you place a wet hat on the counter and the brim is sitting correctly and the dome of the hat isn't caving in, don't mold it. Let it dry just like that and it will turn out fine. But if you have a hat that's too small and needs to be stretched, or its center is caving in, it will have a better and longer-lasting shape if you mold it.

You can also use your fingers to do the molding. You'll be surprised at how much the final look of the piece is altered by how it is shaped when it's damp. Take the Four-in-One Brooch (page 29), for instance. You can finger-press the petals flat and the flower becomes a two-dimensional adornment for any jacket or hat. Use your thumbs to force each petal to curve up and the piled petals take on a sculptural quality.

Household items make useful molds for shaping felted pieces.

PINNING

Pinning is critical for the any flat item with square corners, such as the Calla Lily Clutch (page 49). When the purse comes out of the wash, I finger-press it on the ironing board into a perfect rectangle, then I pin it with standard straight pins along all four sides so that it stays flat and square as it dries. If you don't have an ironing board, you can use any flat surface that will accept pins — like a mattress — as long as the piece stays put after you stretch or press, then pin your work into the right shape.

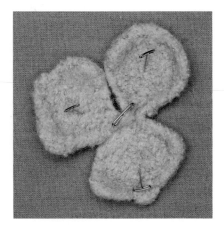

Pin wet felted pieces to hold shape until dry.

Pinning is also helpful when you have an unruly item that wants to pop up or insists on felting unevenly. For instance, I pin each petal on the Tri-Petal Flower Bracelet (page 35) down so the petals don't close in on themselves as they dry.

I also pin the belts because they don't felt evenly. I can stretch and pin the thin areas so they match the thicker areas. If I let them dry like that, the unevenness is eliminated.

SCRUNCHING

Scrunching is when you bunch up the wet material accordion-style and let it dry. I use this technique for any item that has wavy edges, like the Tied Scarf (page 107). The key to success in this technique is to let it dry completely before moving it. Think of rolling slightly damp hair in curlers. The hair will hold its curl longer if it is totally dry before taking the rollers out.

COMPRESSING

Compressing picks up where pinning leaves off. If you have pinned an item that needs to be flat, but it refuses to cooperate and it continues to pop up, try compressing it. This is the technique I use with the Swirl Placemats (page 133). When I first made them, I started by pinning them down, but when I released the pins, the edges curled up. Undaunted, I found an oversized, heavy book and set it on the damp placemats until they were completely dry — about two days. They now lay flat. If they ever begin to curl again, I'll repeat the process.

CLEAN UP, CLEAN UP, EVERYBODY CLEAN UP

The last step in felting is cleaning up the finished product. The phrase "a shave and a haircut" is apropos here because that's basically all you do. I snip off any loose yarns that may have emerged during felting, and if the wool is too fuzzy, I use scissors or a razor to give the surface a little shave.

Where to Start

If you're just starting to knit, try the Tied Scarf (page 107). This is a no-miss pattern that requires no shaping and yields dramatic results every time. If you're a little afraid to throw hours of knitting into a washing machine in the hopes that something good might happen, try the Four-in-One Brooch on page 29. These quick knits may be just the building blocks you need before graduating to bigger projects, like the Falling Leaf Pillow (page 117).

For those of you who love working with color, I've included a couple of Fair Isle knits: the Groovy Flower Purse (page 71) and the Petals & Stems Purse (page 57). For the adventurous among you, the Night Star Wrap (page 99) is an elegant shawl that breaks just about every knitting rule; but when it's done, you'll be the proud owner of a one-of-a-kind pairing for your little black dress.

As you work through these projects, you'll find that felting is an almost magical experience. I hope the patterns I've included here will be the starting point for your own obsession with felting — if you don't have one already.

As you pull out your needles and begin clicking away, be confident that what's coming off those size 10s (12s, 14s . . .) *will* eventually turn into the cute little number you see in the photo.

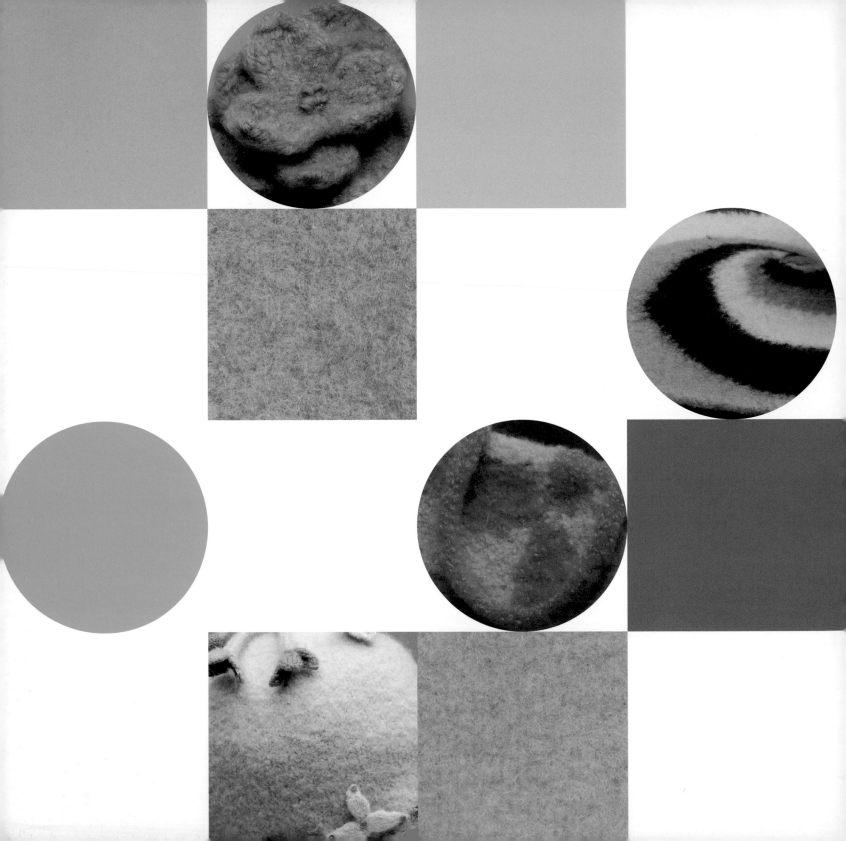

Pick Up and Knit

It's now time to pick up those needles and get to the fun part — your projects! If you get nervous, refer back to the important tips in the preceding pages. If something goes wrong, flip to the troubleshooting guide (page 21). If you're too afraid to throw, say, the Petals & Stems Purse into the washer, give My Basic Felting Technique a reread for a little reassurance. Now you have the moxie to do it — so relax, have fun, and enjoy the knitting and felting!

Four-in-One Brooch

With your imagination and these little brooches, the possibilities abound. Pin one on a hat. Fan two out over a pillow. Attach three to a barrette and clip it behind your ear. These highly versatile, adjustable brooches are as fun to experiment with as they are to knit. Great for a quick first-time felting project because they guarantee success. *Warning:* You can't knit just one!

FINISHED MEASUREMENTS
Approximately 3"–3½" (7.5–9 cm) in diameter

YARN
Knit Picks, Merino Style, 100% Merino wool, DK weight, 123 yds (112 m)/ 1¾ oz (50 g)

     Petal 23449, 1 ball
     Honey 23448, 1 ball
     Asparagus 23451, 1 ball
     Rhubarb 23443, 1 ball

Knit Picks, Wool of the Andes, 100% Peruvian Highland Wool, worsted weight, 110 yds (100.5 m)/1¾ oz (50 g)

     Rain 23768, 1 ball

NEEDLES
US #10 (6 mm) straight needles

GAUGE
Any worsted-weight or DK-weight wool that will felt should yield the correct proportions, no matter your tension. The lighter weight yarns will create less bulky flowers.

OTHER SUPPLIES
Yarn needle

PLAN OF ACTION
You begin each flower by casting on 15 stitches in color of your choice, working in stockinette stitch (knit 1 row, purl 1 row) for 2 rows. You then work one petal at a time using just 5 of the 15 stitches for each of the 3 petals. You finish with a pile of French knots in the center.

When you are ready to felt, shrink the flowers until their stitches disappear. The more you wash, the stiffer they get and the easier they are to mold into real-life-looking flowers.

KNITTING THE SMALL FLOWER

SET UP Cast on 15 stitches.

ROW 1 Knit to end of row.

ROW 2 Purl to end of row.

Petal 1

NOTE Use the first 5 stitches on the needle only. Turn at the end of each row.

ROW 1 K1, Inc 1, K1, Inc 1, K1. Turn. *You now have* 7 stitches.

ROW 2 P1, Inc 1, P1, Inc 1, P1, Inc 1, P1. Turn. *You now have* 10 stitches.

ALL INCREASES ARE NOT THE SAME

Most people learn just one way to increase when they begin knitting, but there are several techniques to choose from; each is used for a different reason. Some increases disappear into the work completely, others leave their mark on the front of the work. Some slant in one direction, some in the other. Because stitch definition disappears in felting, I never worry about whether my increases are visible or slanting properly. My concern is more about what the increases do in terms of shaping the work. Unless otherwise noted, use the bar increase in all patterns in this book.

The **bar increase** earned its name because it leaves a little bar at the front of the work. This handy marking helps you to keep track of your increases as you knit. To execute it on knit rows, you make two stitches out of one by knitting into the front and back of a stitch before dropping it off the needle. (For increases on purl rows, purl into the front and back of each stitch.)

Bar Increase

Step 1

Step 2

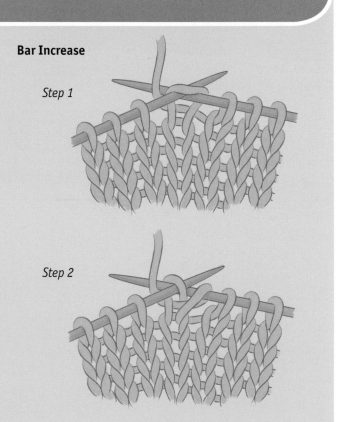

ROW 3 K1, K2tog, K1, K2tog, K1, K2tog, K1. Turn. *You now have* 7 stitches.

ROW 4 P1, P2tog, P1, P2tog, P1. Turn. *You now have* 5 stitches.

ROW 5 K2tog 2 times, K1. Turn. *You now have* 3 stitches.

ROW 6 Bind off in purl, break yarn, draw end through last stitch and pull. Break yarn.

Petal 2

NOTE In this section, use the next 5 stitches on the needle. Pick up a new strand of yarn to begin.

Repeat Rows 1–6 of Petal 1.

Petal 3

NOTE In this section, use the remaining 5 stitches on the needle. Pick up a new strand of yarn to begin.

Repeat Rows 1–6 of Petal 1.

Weave in all ends.

KNITTING THE MEDIUM FLOWER

SET UP Cast on 15 stitches.

ROW 1 Knit to end of row.

ROW 2 Purl to end of row.

Petal 1

NOTE Use the first 5 stitches on the needle only. Turn at the end of each row.

ROW 1 K1, Inc 1, K1, Inc 1, K1. Turn. *You now have* 7 stitches.

ROW 2 P1, Inc 1, P1, Inc 1, P1, Inc 1, P1. Turn. *You now have* 10 stitches.

ROW 3 K1, Inc 1, K6, Inc 1, K1. Turn. *You now have* 12 stitches.

ROW 4 P1, P2tog, P2, P2tog. P2, P2tog, P1. Turn. *You now have* 9 stitches.

ROW 5 K1, K2tog, K1, K2tog, K2tog, K1. Turn. *You now have* 6 stitches.

ROW 6 P2tog 3 times. *You now have* 3 stitches.

ROW 7 K2tog, K1. *You now have* 2 stitches.

ROW 8 Bind off in purl, break yarn, draw end through last stitch and pull.

Petal 2

NOTE In this section, use the next 5 stitches on the needle. Pick up a new strand of yarn to begin.

Repeat Rows 1–8 of Petal 1.

Petal 3

NOTE In this section, use the remaining 5 stitches on the needle. Pick up a new strand of yarn to begin.

Repeat Rows 1–8 of Petal 1.

Weave in all ends.

KNITTING THE LARGE FLOWER

SET UP Cast on 15 stitches.

ROW 1 Knit to end of row.

ROW 2 Purl to end of row.

Petal 1

NOTE Use the first 5 stitches on the needle only. Turn at the end of each row.

ROW 1 K1, Inc 1, K1, Inc 1, K1. Turn. *You now have* 7 stitches.

ROW 2 P1, Inc 1, P1, Inc 1, P1, Inc 1, P1. Turn. *You now have* 10 stitches.

ROW 3 K1, Inc 1, K6, Inc 1, K1. Turn. *You now have* 12 stitches.

ROW 4 P1, Inc 1, P4, Inc 1, P3, Inc 1, P1. Turn. *You now have* 15 stitches.

ROW 5 Knit to end of row. Turn.

ROW 6 P1, P2tog, P4, P2tog, P3, P2tog, P1. Turn. *You now have* 12 stitches.

ROW 7 K1, K2tog, K2, K2tog, K2, K2tog, K1. Turn. *You now have* 9 stitches.

ROW 8 P1, P2tog, P1, P2tog, P2tog, P1. Turn. *You now have* 6 stitches.

ROW 9 K2tog 3 times. Turn. *You now have* 3 stitches.

GROW A ROSE

Cultivate a rose from the Four-in-One Brooch by taking advantage of felted wool's shaping capabilities. Wet wool is almost like clay. You can mold it into any position, and once it's dry, it holds its shape. Here's how to make a rose:

1 Knit one of each flower size (small, medium, and large) all in the same color.

2 Felt as instructed.

3 While the pieces are still wet, use your fingers to force each of the petals into the curved shape of an actual petal, then cup the petals toward each other so they meet in the center. Tie loosely with a strand of yarn so they hold their position. Allow them to dry completely.

4 Lay the 3 flowers on top of one another, with the largest on the bottom and the smallest on top. Join with a same-color French knot in the center.

ROW 10 P2tog, P1. Turn. *You now have* 2 stitches.

ROW 11 Bind off stitches, break yarn, draw end through last stitch and pull. Break yarn.

Petal 2

NOTE In this section, use the next 5 stitches on the needle. Pick up a new strand of yarn to begin.

Repeat Rows 1–11 of Petal 1.

Petal 3

NOTE In this section, use the remaining 5 stitches on the needle. Pick up a new strand of yarn to begin.

Repeat Rows 1–11 of Petal 1.

FINISHING THE FLOWERS

Thread a yarn needle with MC. Using a running stitch, sew along the base of the three petals. Tightly pull both ends of yarn to gather, until the petals come together in the center. Tie off tightly and weave in the ends.

FELTING

Place the flowers in a mesh bag or a pillowcase so they don't get lost in the washing machine. Felt the pieces individually, before putting them together. Following My Basic Felting Technique on page 16.

FINISHING

Shape as desired and let dry. When the petal groupings have dried, mix and match until you find the combinations you like.

Adorn the centers with French knots. Try using one knot, or pile the knots high to create the look of a sunflower's center. (See Anatomy of a French Knot, below.) Play around until you settle on your favorite styling!

ANATOMY OF A FRENCH KNOT

1 Thread a yarn needle with an 18" (45.5 cm) length of yarn, either matching or contrasting.

2 Insert the needle up through the center of the flower from the wrong side, and pull the yarn through, leaving a tail about 6" (15 cm) long.

3 Wrap the yarn around the needle counter-clockwise three or four times.

4 Insert the needle back through the flower, entering the fabric close to, but not right into the hole you came through in Step 2. Hold the wrapped yarn in place on the needle as you draw the needle back to the wrong side.

5 Pull on both tails to tighten the knot, and then tie them together twice to fasten securely. Weave in ends and trim.

Tri-Petal Flower Bracelet

Who knew that felting could be this delicate? Worked on US #2 (2.75 mm) needles in fingering weight yarn, this dainty bracelet is built from a solid I-cord band base. Stitches for the flowers are picked up and knit, connecting the flowers to the band. Beads are sewn on after the bracelet is felted and dried.

FINISHED MEASUREMENTS

Approximately 7¾" (20 cm) long, 1¼" (3 cm) wide

YARN

Knit Picks Palette, 100% wool, fingering weight, 231 yds (211 m)/1¾ oz (50 g)

CA   Tan 23736, 1 ball
CB   Blush 23718, 1 ball

NEEDLES

Set of US #2 (2.75 mm) double-point needles

GAUGE

Any fingering weight wool yarn should yield the correct proportions, no matter your tension. The bracelet's final size can be adjusted when attaching the hardware after felting.

OTHER SUPPLIES

Split-ring stitch markers
Straight pins
2 ribbon crimps
1 lobster claw clasp
1 jump ring
Small beads, 6 per flower
Beading thread and needle
Needle-nose pliers

PLAN OF ACTION

The bracelet is created by first knitting an I-cord. As you knit, you place eight stitch markers to indicate where you will later pick up stitches for the flower petals.

Once felted, the flowers are pinned down to dry to ensure they hold their shape.

KNITTING THE I-CORD

NOTE   For I-cord, see What's an I-Cord? on page 55.

SET UP   Using CA, cast on 2 stitches.

ROW 1   Knit both stitches.

ROW 2   Without turning work, slide stitches across needle. Pull yarn tightly from end of row behind needle and knit both stitches.

ROWS 3–71   Repeat Row 2, placing a marker every eighth row with seven rows left at the end. Bind off and weave in end. You will have 8 markers.

KNITTING A FLOWER

NOTE   For the increases, knit into the front and back of a stitch to make two stitches. (See All Increases Are Not the Same on page 30.)

NOTE   Knit Flower 1 in CB and Flower 2 in CA. Continue alternating the color of the flowers for the remainder of the pattern. Use your double-point needles as you would straight needles to knit the flowers.

Petal 1

SET UP   Pick up 2 stitches at the first stitch marker.

ROW 1   Using CA, knit 2 stitches.

ROW 2   Inc 1 twice purlwise. *You now have* 4 stitches.

ROW 3   Inc 1, K2, Inc 1. *You now have* 6 stitches.

ROW 4   Inc 1, P4, Inc 1. *You now have* 8 stitches.

ROW 5   Knit to end of row.

ROW 6   P2tog, P4, P2tog. *You now have* 6 stitches.

ROW 7   K2tog, K2, K2tog. *You now have* 4 stitches.

ROW 8   P2tog twice. *You now have* 2 stitches.

Bind off and weave in ends.

Petal 2

SET UP   Arrange work so that the first petal is right side facing. Pick up the two stitches at the first row of the petal from the right side.

ROW 1   Using CA, Inc 1 twice. *You now have* 4 stitches.

ROW 2   Inc 1, P2, Inc 1. *You now have* 6 stitches.

ROW 3   Inc 1, K4, Inc 1. *You now have* 8 stitches.

ROW 4   Purl to end of row.

ROW 5   K2tog, K4, K2tog. *You now have* 6 stitches.

ROW 6   P2tog, P2, P2tog. *You now have* 4 stitches.

ROW 7   K2tog twice. *You now have* 2 stitches.

Bind off in purl and weave in ends.

Petal 3

Pick up 1 stitch at the first row of each of the two petals, right sides facing. Create another petal in the same manner as you did the second petal. The petals will twist awkwardly, but once the piece is felted and blocked and the center beads are sewn on, they'll fan out and take on the appearance of real flowers.

ADDITIONAL FLOWERS

Continue on, working a flower at each marker until you have eight flowers alternating in color.

Weave in any loose ends.

FELTING

Follow My Basic Felting Technique on page 16. The bracelet will take a long time to felt, and the stitches will never fully disappear. You can speed up the process by adding jeans to the wash.

NOTE Because the bracelet is so small, I suggest you place it in a mesh laundry bag or a pillowcase so you don't lose it under the washing machine's agitator. The mesh bag or pillowcase also provides more agitation, which is important with this bracelet. Because it is small and made with fingering yarn, it doesn't respond to agitation the way larger pieces do and thus may not felt completely.

BLOCKING

While the bracelet is still wet, lay it on a towel. The petal tips tend to fold up, so you'll have to splay, finger-press, and pin each one in place, then let the piece dry completely.

SEWING ON THE BEADS

When the bracelet is completely dry, use a beading needle and matching sewing thread to sew beads onto each petal tip and in the center of each petal.

ADDING THE CLASP

If necessary, cut the I-cord to get the right fit. Squeeze a ribbon crimp onto both ends of the I-cord band using needle-nose pliers. Attach the jump ring on one end and the lobster claw clasp on the other, as shown below.

Star Choker

Felting has gotten a bad rap as yielding a stiff, scratchy fabric suitable only for making bags and slippers. Not so! When paired with something other than worsted wool and size 10 needles, felting can create the most surprising of items, like this delicate choker.

FINISHED MEASUREMENTS
Band (not including I-cord closure): 1" (2.5 cm) wide and 13" (33 cm) long

YARN
Knit Picks Palette, 100% Peruvian wool, fingering weight, 231 yds (211 m)/1¾ oz (50 g)
CA   Wood 23734, 1 ball
CB   Fawn 23735, 1 ball

NEEDLES
US #2 (2.75 mm) straight needles
Set of US #2 (2.75 mm) double-point needles

GAUGE
Since this item will be felted and it has a long I-cord closure that is secured like a ribbon, it should fit any size neck, regardless of your tension. Any fingering weight wool yarn worked on US #2 (2.75 mm) needles will suffice.

OTHER SUPPLIES
Stitch holders
Yarn needle
Small beads
Beading thread and needle

PLAN OF ACTION
This pattern is worked by knitting four tips of a star, placing them on a holder, then knitting them together as intarsia following a quick decrease pattern for the star's center. These stars are joined together at their points to form a five-star band, with half stars at each end. I-cords picked up from the half stars serve as ties.

KNITTING THE FIRST STAR TIP

NOTE For the increases, knit into the front and back of a stitch to make two stitches. (See All Increases Are Not the Same on page 30.)

SET UP Using CA, cast on 1 stitch, leaving a 6" (15 cm) tail.

ROW 1 Knit.

ROWS 2, 4, 6, AND 8 Purl.

ROW 3 Inc 1. *You now have* 2 stitches.

ROW 5 Inc 1 twice. *You now have* 4 stitches.

ROW 7 Inc 1, K2, Inc 1. *You now have* 6 stitches.

Measure a tail that is 15" (38 cm) long, and break yarn. You will use this tail to work the center of the star later. Slide stitches onto a stitch holder.

Star Tip 2

Using CB, create another star tip by repeating Rows 1–8. Leave a measured tail. Slide stitches onto a holder.

Star Tips 3 and 4

Create two more star tips, one each of CA and CB. As you finish each tip, slide it onto a holder.

Star Center Decrease Pattern

NOTE The center intarsia pattern is worked with the long tails located at the right side of each star tip. (See Intarsia on page 143.) At this point, none of the star tips are joined. As you work your first row of the decrease pattern below, join the star tips together by securely twisting the yarns of each color around each other on the wrong side.

SET UP Slide stitches from holder onto the needle so the star-tip colors are alternating and the first star tip you will knit is CB. *You now have* 24 stitches.

ROW 1 * Using CB tail of first star, K2, K2tog, K2. Change to CA tail of second star, and remembering to twist yarn K2, K2tog, K2; repeat from * to end of row. *You now have* 20 stitches.

ROW 2 * Using CA, P2, P2tog, P1. Change to CB, P2, P2tog, P1; repeat from * to end of row. *You now have* 16 stitches.

ROW 3 * Using CB, K1, K2tog, K1. Change to CA, K1, K2tog, K1; repeat from * to end of row. *You now have* 12 stitches.

ROW 4 * Using CA, P1, P2tog. Change to CB, P1, P2tog; repeat from * to end of row. *You now have* 8 stitches.

ROW 5 * Using CB, K2tog. Change to CA, K2tog; repeat from * to end of row. *You now have 4 stitches.*

Weave tail from the last stitch back through the remaining four stitches on your needle. Pull tight (like a purse string). Tie two tails together into a secure knot at the fabric surface in the middle of the star. Repeat with the remaining tails. The knots will prevent holes from forming during felting, disappearing in the process. (See Walking on the Wild Side on page 100.) Using matching yarn and a yarn needle, seam the two sides together from this center point out to the point at which the decrease pattern begins to form into a four-point star. Weave in the ends at the middle of the star, but leaving the ends at the points. You'll use these ends later.

Make five stars altogether. (The necklace is made up of five whole stars and two half stars.)

KNITTING THE HALF STARS AND I-CORDS

Two half stars with I-cords attached to them go at each end of the choker band. (See What's an I-Cord? on page 55.)

Make two star tips, one in each color. Join them together using the decrease pattern, but skip the repeats, because you have only half as many stitches. The completed half star is shaped like an arrow. Knot the pair of ends. Create another half star, making sure that the color order of your star tips is identical to the one you just completed.

ROW 1 Using CB yarn and double-point needles, pick up and knit 2 stitches at the point of the arrow.

ROW 2 Without turning work, slide stitches to other end of double-point needle and K2, giving yarn a little tug after you've knit the first stitch.

ROWS 3–60 Repeat Row 2.

Repeat for the second half star.

PUTTING THE PIECES TOGETHER

Using a yarn needle, sew the points of the first half star to the opposite color points of a whole star: Thread the tail at the end of each point into the top of the other point. After, tie tails in a close double knot on the wrong side before weaving them in.

Attach the remaining four stars to the full star in the same manner to form the band, then attach the second half star.

FELTING AND FINISHING

Place the choker in a mesh laundry bag or pillow-case so it doesn't get lost under the agitator. Follow My Basic Felting Technique on page 16. The choker takes a long time to felt and the stitches never fully disappear. Finger-press while damp into shape.

When the necklace is completely dry, use a beading needle and thread to sew beads to the center of each star, at each intersection between stars, and to the ends of the I-cord closures.

A Trio of Belts

These belts range in difficulty from extra easy to extra hard. The Simple Stripes Belt is the easiest. It is knit in stockinette stitch with color changes in every row. The Check-This Belt is slightly more difficult, but it's a good introduction to intarsia. With four colors in play at once in a complex Fair Isle pattern, the Inverted C Belt is for those who like a challenge. Because Fair Isle knitting involves carrying strands of yarn along the back of the piece as you work across the rows, the Inverted C Belt is weighty and sturdy, making it a perfect match with jeans.

FINISHED MEASUREMENTS
(See Plan of Action at right)

YARN
Peruvian Collection Highland Wool, 100% wool, worsted weight, 109 yds (100 m)/1.75 oz (50 g)

CA	Pottery Red 2120, 1 ball	
CB	Dusty Rose 2507, 1 ball	
CC	Rose Pink 7132, 1 ball	
CD	Claret 2020, 1 ball	

NEEDLES
For the Simple Stripes Belt and the Inverted C Belt
One US #10 (6 mm) circular needle, 24" (60 cm) long
For the Check-This Belt
US #10 (6 mm) straight needles

GAUGE
Any worsted-weight wool should yield the correct proportions, no matter your tension.

OTHER SUPPLIES
Crochet hook, optional (for making belt loops)
Bobbins, optional (for winding the separate balls for intarsia)
Yarn needle
Straight pins

PLAN OF ACTION
Because belts need to fit just right, I've written these patterns so the belts will turn out extra-long. After they are felted, you can cut them to the correct size for your frame. Usually cutting knitted items is unheard of, as the pieces would unravel within minutes. But cutting is a viable option for felted knits because they won't unravel and the raw edge is easily disguised by hemming down on the backside or with stitchery, such as a blanket or overcast stitch. Rather than fuss with nailing the perfect stitch count for the size, sometimes it's easier to knit oversize and slice. How naughty to cut knitting!

KNITTING THE SIMPLE STRIPES BELT

NOTE The stripes are created by working one row of each of the four colors in alternation as indicated below and in the chart on page 47. Work the entire belt in stockinette stitch: I suggest using circulars so it's easier to manage the large number of cast-on stitches, but you will knit back and forth on the circulars as you would straight needles. Break yarn after each row and weave in end.

SET UP Using CD and the circular needle, cast on 200 stitches.

ROW 1 Using CA, knit to end of row.

ROW 2 Using CB, purl to end of row.

ROW 3 Using CC, knit to end of row.

ROW 4 Using CD, purl to end of row.

ROWS 5–8 Repeat Rows 1–4.

ROW 9 Using CA, knit to end of row.

ROW 10 Using CB, purl to end of row.

ROW 11 Using CC, knit to end of row.

Using CD, bind off in purl. Weave in end.

KNITTING THE CHECK-THIS BELT

NOTE This belt is knit widthwise in stockinette stitch, following the chart on page 47. Work the pattern as intarsia except on the rows where the checks shift. For instance, this is how you would work Row 7: To begin knitting, use the CC strand that is one color block away by pulling it across the back of the three CA stitches. For each new color block, use the yarn three stitches away. As you work, carry the CA yarn from the first color block with you. That way, when it's time to knit the last color block, the CD yarn is in the right place. Use this technique each time the color blocks shift.

SET UP Using CA, cast on 16 stitches.

ROW 1 Knit to end of row, following Check-This Chart on page 47, beginning at the bottom right.

ROW 2 Purl to end of row, continuing to follow the chart, this time reading from left to right.

ROWS 3–24 Repeat Rows 1 and 2.

NEXT ROWS Repeat Rows 1–24 (on the chart) 7 more times.

Using CD, bind off. Weave in all ends.

KNITTING THE INVERTED C BELT

NOTE This belt is knit lengthwise. Following the chart on page 47, work the pattern in Fair Isle, carrying colors not in use across the back as you proceed. (See Fair Isle and Felting on page 45.) With the exception of Rows 6, 7, and 8, don't twist the yarns around each other each time you change color, as this will make the pattern too hard to work. Work the entire belt in stockinette stitch: Knit rows start on the right; purl rows start on the left. The chart shows the 8-stitch pattern, which is repeated 36 times in each row.

SET UP   Using CD and the circular needle, cast on 288 stitches.

ROW 1   Knit to end of row, following Inverted C Chart on page 47, beginning at the bottom right. Repeat the 8-stitch pattern across the row 36 times.

ROW 2   Purl to end of row, continuing to follow the chart, this time reading from left to right.

ROWS 3–12   Continuing in stockinette stitch (knit 1 row, purl 1 row), complete the chart.

FAIR ISLE AND FELTING

When knitting in the Fair Isle style, you carry the colors not in use across the back of your work. This can present a problem in felting because the carried yarn has a tendency to felt faster than the knit yarn. The result: The pattern at the front can pucker. To prevent this, leave a lot of slack as you carry the yarns along the back. If you find your work is puckering when it felts, pull it out of the machine and stretch it aggressively. If the piece has felted to the point that it won't unravel if you cut into it, you can even snip the carried yarns and stretch it again. This technique has helped me save many a Fair Isle project gone awry.

Using CD, bind off. Weave in all ends. Any ruffling in the bind-off row will resolve during felting.

KNITTING THE BOBBLE

NOTE   Make 2 bobbles for the Simple Stripes Belt and 2 bobbles for the Check-This Belt.

SET UP   Using CD for the Simple Stripes Belt or CA for the Check-This Belt, cast on 12 stitches, leaving a 10-inch (25 cm) tail.

ROW 1   Knit to end of row.

ROW 2   Purl to end of row.

ROW 3   K2tog to end of the row. *You now have 6 stitches.*

ROW 4   P2tog to the end of the row. *You now have 3 stitches.*

Break yarn, leaving a 12" (36 cm) tail, and thread tail into a yarn needle.

FINISH   Remove remaining 3 stitches from needle, and thread tail back through stitches. Pull tight (like a purse string), and then seam the two sides together so the piece becomes a small cone. Still using the same threaded needle, pick up each stitch along the cast-on edge. Stuff cast-on tail into the center and draw tail through the stitches. Pull tight so the circle gathers into a little ball. Sew hole closed and weave in ends.

MAKING THE BELT LOOPS

NOTE   For the Check-This Belt, make one 3" (7.5 cm) crochet chain. For the Inverted C Belt, make two 3½" (8.75 cm) crochet chains. (See Spirals by Hand on page 68.)

FELTING THE BELTS

Place the bobbles and crochet chains in a mesh laundry bag, so you don't lose them during the felting. Follow My Basic Felting Technique on page 16. As the belt felts, check it regularly to make sure it isn't tangling on itself. If it is, pull it out, untangle it, then put it back until felted as desired.

BLOCKING

It's important to block these belts to keep their sides from curling up. Lay them flat on a towel. (You may need two towels to get enough length.) Place on a surface that you can pin, like an ironing board or a mattress. Pin all the way along the edges. Let dry completely.

FINISHING

Simple Stripes Belt

This belt is meant to be tied at the waist with the bobble ends hanging in front, so don't shorten the belt. Using CD threaded in a yarn needle, wrap the last 2" (5 cm) of each end of the belt with yarn. Pack the yarn close together, and wrap it tightly. Leave a small amount of the belt protruding at the tip. Secure the wrap by threading the yarn

back through the layers several times. Trim the protruding fabric so the top of the wrap is flat. Using yarn needle and matching yarn, sew the bobbles to the top as shown below.

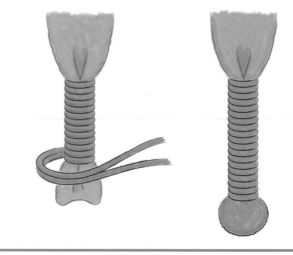

Check-This Belt

SET UP   Size belt to wearer and cut both ends, leaving room for hems.

BOBBLE   Center a bobble on one side of the belt, about ½" (1 cm) from the end. Using a yarn needle and matching yarn, sew securely in place.

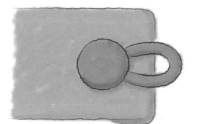

LOOP Fold the raw edges to the back and stitch in place. Center the crocheted loop under one of the bobbles; adjust size so it fits over the other bobble. Using a yarn needle and matching yarn, sew securely through all layers.

Inverted C Belt

Before cutting this belt, notice how the closure requires the ends to overlap. Size the belt to wearer and cut both ends, leaving enough room for the overlap and a hem for each end. Fold the raw edges to the back and sew in place. Place the crochet chains in the appropriate place for your size and using a yarn needle and matching yarn, sew them securely to the back.

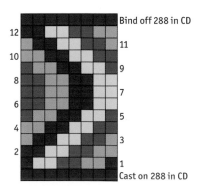

Check-This Chart

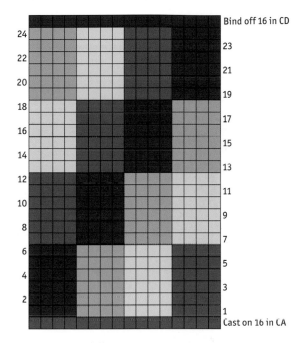

Bind off 16 in CD

Cast on 16 in CA

Simple Stripes Chart

Note: When working all charts, knit rows start on the right and purl rows start on the left.

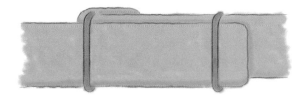

- ■ CA Pottery Red
- ■ CB Dusty Rose
- ■ CC Rose Pink
- ■ CD Claret

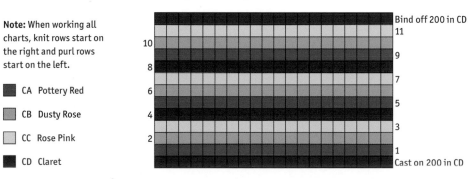

Bind off 200 in CD

Cast on 200 in CD

Inverted C Chart

Bind off 288 in CD

Cast on 288 in CD

Calla Lily Clutch

This little black evening clutch earns its *wow!* factor through the addition of a dramatic calla lily adornment. The pattern is straightforward stockinette stitch, but when you place the I-cord piping, you'll find a surprising (and fun!) knitting challenge.

FINISHED MEASUREMENTS

Before felting: 11" (28 cm) long and 8½" (21.5 cm) high
After felting: 10½" (26.5 cm) long and 5½" (14 cm) high

YARN

Cascade 220, 100% wool, 220 yards (201 m)/3.5oz (100 g)

MC	Black 8555, 2 skeins
CA	Highland Green 9430, 1 skein
CB	Lime Heather 9461, 1 skein
CC	Celery 9407, 1 skein
CD	Natural 8010, 1 skein
CE	California Poppy 7826, about 3 yards (2.75 m)

NEEDLES

US #10 (6 mm) straight needles
A spare set of smaller-size straight needles (for the three-needle bind off)
Set US #10 (6 mm) double-point needles

GAUGE

Any worsted-weight wool should yield the correct proportions, no matter your tension.

OTHER SUPPLIES

Yarn needle
Split-ring stitch markers
Stitch holders
Point protectors
Straight pins

PLAN OF ACTION

The purse is knit in two panels, then joined at the side and bottom edges using a three-needle bind-off. Next, you will pick up stitches from the I-cord piping to knit the calla lily. Be careful to choose a white that will felt when selecting yarn. I suggest doing a test swatch if you use a brand other than Cascade 220.

NOTE For the increases, knit into the front and back of a stitch to make 2 stitches. (See All Increases Are Not the Same on page 30.)

Front Panel

SET UP Using larger straight needles and MC, cast on 40 stitches.

ROWS 1–6 Work in stockinette stitch (knit one row, purl one row).

ROW 7 Knit, and increase 1 stitch in the middle of the row. *You now have* 41 stitches.

ROW 8 Purl, and increase 1 stitch in the middle of the row. *You now have* 42 stitches.

ROWS 9 AND 10 Repeat Rows 7 and 8. *You now have* 44 stitches.

ROW 11 Repeat Row 7. *You now have* 45 stitches.

ROWS 12–42 Work in stockinette stitch.

Slide stitches onto a holder for later use. Break yarn.

Top Flap and Back Panel

SET UP Using MC, cast on 42 stitches.

ROWS 1–36 Work in stockinette stitch.

ROW 37 Purl this knit row through the back loop to create a turning ridge.

ROW 38 P2tog, purl to the last 2 stitches, P2tog. *You now have* 40 stitches.

ROWS 39–44 Work in stockinette stitch.

ROW 45 Knit, and increase 1 stitch in the middle of the row. *You now have* 41 stitches.

ROW 46 Purl, and increase 1 stitch in the middle of the row. *You now have* 42 stitches.

ROWS 47 AND 48 Repeat Rows 45 and 46. *You now have* 44 stitches.

ROW 49 Repeat Row 45. *You now have* 45 stitches.

ROWS 50–80 Work in stockinette stitch.

Slide stitches onto a holder for later use. Break yarn.

I-CORD PIPING

SET UP Using two double-point needles and CA, cast on 4 stitches. (See What's an I-Cord? on page 55.)

ROW 1 Knit to end of row.

ROW 2 Without turning work, slide stitches across needle. Pull yarn tightly from end of row behind needle and knit all the stitches.

ROWS 3–117 Repeat Row 2.

Don't bind off. Place the stitches on a holder to be used later as the stem for the calla lily.

PICKING UP STITCHES DEMYSTIFIED

I always get a little nervous when I'm following a pattern and it instructs me to pick up stitches. What, exactly, does this mean? Do I pull up a loop or introduce a new yarn to make a stitch? Do I pick up the stitches on the very edge or one row in? Because felting is so forgiving, picking up stitches no longer needs to invoke such hand-wringing. Here are some general rules when picking up stitches in felting:

● Don't introduce a new yarn when picking up stitches for felted items. The reason for introducing a new yarn in regular knitting is so the finished work won't gap or pull along edges where stitches have been picked up. All gapping and pulling resolves during felting. Voilà, problem solved!

● Pick up the stitches on the outermost edge. Yes, this causes holes between the edge and whatever will be added on, but again, it doesn't matter because felting melds everything together.

● Pick up exactly the number of stitches specified in patterns. Most patterns are very specific about the number of stitches to pick up along an edge. This is because felted knits shrink more in length than they do in width — meaning that knit-on borders shrink at a different rate than the rest of the work. One way felting designers accommodate this little quirk is to pick up what seems like an unusual number of stitches along borders — if they dare add borders at all!

ATTACHING I-CORD PIPING AND SEAMING PURSE EDGES

The three-needle bind off is used to turn the I-cord into piping around the edges of the purse. (In this case, it's actually a four-needle bind off.) You first pick up stitches from each of the three pieces (front panel, I-cord, and back panel), then knit a stitch from each of the pieces together, binding off as you work. The process is done in three steps, starting with the left side seam, then the bottom seam, and finally the right side seam. (See Three-Needle Bind-Off Method on page 65.) Use double-point needles and point protectors to prevent your stitches from slipping off the needles.

Step 1: Left Side Seam

Using a double-point needle, pick up 36 stitches lengthwise along the I-cord, starting at the cast-on stitch and working your way up. With a split-ring marker, mark the 37th stitch. Pick up one stitch for each row and don't skip any stitches.

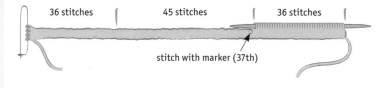

36 stitches 45 stitches 36 stitches

stitch with marker (37th)

Next, arrange your work so it looks like the illustration below. Back panel is wrong-side facing and front panel is right-side facing. With a second double-point needle, pick up 36 stitches along the left side seam of the front panel. With a third double-point needle, pick up 36 stitches along the left side seam of the back panel (wrong-side facing). *Tip:* You will get 36 stitches by picking up 5 stitches and skipping 1.

left side seams

Next, rearrange your work to orient the right (knit) sides of both front and back panels facing each other. Place the double-point needle with the I-cord stitches in between the front and back panels.

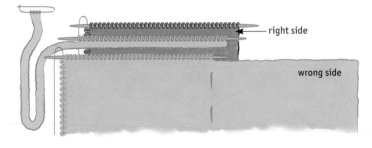

Starting at the turning ridge, with a fourth double-point needle and new MC yarn, knit each of the first stitches on all three needles together. Knit the second stitch on all three needles. Bind off the first stitch. Repeat until you have knit and bound off 35 stitches. Leave the last stitch on the needle.

Step 2: Bottom Seam

Slide the 45 stitches of the front panel from the holder onto a double-point needle. Slide the 45 stitches of the back panel onto a second double-point needle. Starting at the split ring marker, pick up 45 stitches lengthwise along the I-cord in the same row you used for the first side seam so the cord doesn't twist. Pick up one stitch for each row and don't skip any stitches (see illustration above). The panels' right sides are facing each other. Place the needle with the I-cord stitches in between them. Knit all three together as you did with the side seam. Bind off as you work, starting with the stitch still on your needle. Continue binding off until 1 stitch remains. Leave the last stitch on the needle.

Step 3: Right Side Seam

Join the right side seams as you did the left, by picking up 36 stitches along the I-cord (see the illustration under step 1), 36 stitches along the front panel right seam, and 36 stitches along the back panel right seam. The right sides of the panels are facing each other. Place the needle with the I-cord stitches in between them. Knit all three together. Bind off using the stitch still on your needle. Continue binding off until 1 stitch remains. Break yarn and draw the tail back through the last stitch. Weave in end. Turn the bag right side out (wrong sides facing each other).

KNITTING THE CALLA LILY

NOTE For the increases, knit into the front and the back of a stitch to make 2 stitches. (See All Increases Are Not the Same on page 30.)

Stem

SET UP Place the four I-cord stitches from the holder onto a double-point needle.

With CA, K1, Inc 1, K2. *You now have* 5 stitches.

Without turning work, slide stitches across needle. Pull the yarn from the end of row and K2, Inc 1, K2. *You now have* 6 stitches.

NOTE In the next few rows you will gradually add two lighter shades of green to create a gradation as the stem gives way to the flower. As you add the lighter greens, you'll also be increasing. To begin, you have six green stitches on your needle.

Continue sliding stitches across the needle at the end of each row, since you are still making an I-cord. *Note:* When you start adding colors, it gets a little tricky. Every time you slide your stitches over to begin a new row, remember to pull the yarn of the color that is in use *under* the colors not being knit. The colors (including the tails) not being knit will travel up the center of the I-cord. It will look sloppy and there will be lots of gaps, but after it's felted, it will be beautiful!

ROW 1 K2 CA, K2 CB, K2 CA.

ROW 2 K1 CA, K4 CB, K1 CA.

ROW 3 Using CA, begin Inc 1 by knitting in the front of the stitch, switch to CB and complete increase by knitting in the back of the stitch. Then, K1 CB, K2 CC, K1 CB. In the last stitch, using CB, begin Inc 1 by knitting in the front of the stitch, switch to CA and complete increase by knitting in the back of the stitch. *You now have* 8 stitches. Break CA yarn.

ROW 4 Using CB, Inc 1, K1 CB, K3 CC, K2 CB, Inc 1. *You now have* 10 stitches.

ROW 5 Using CB, Inc 1, K7 CC, K1 CB, Inc 1. *You now have* 12 stitches.

ROW 6 K1 CB, K11 CC. Break CB yarn.

ROW 7 K1 CC, K2 CD, K6 CC, K3 CD.

ROW 8 K4 CD, K4 CC, K4 CD.

ROW 9 K5 CD, K2 CC, K5 CD. Break CC yarn. With a yarn needle, weave all the ends back into the center of the cord.

Flower

From here on, work the pattern as if your double-point needles were straight needles, turning your work after each row. Work in stockinette stitch with CD only. To begin, orient work so that the purl side faces you.

ROW 1 Purl to end of row.

ROW 2 Cast on 2 stitches. Knit to end of row. *You now have* 14 stitches.

ROW 3 Cast on 2 stitches. Purl to end of row. *You now have* 16 stitches.

ROW 4 Cast on 2 stitches. Knit to end of row. *You now have* 18 stitches.

ROW 5 Cast on 2 stitches. Purl to end of row. *You now have* 20 stitches.

ROW 6 K1, Inc 1, knit until 2 stitches remain, Inc 1, K1. *You now have* 22 stitches.

ROW 7 Purl to end of row.

ROWS 8–15 Repeat Rows 6 and 7 four times. *You now have* 30 stitches.

ROWS 16–23 Work in stockinette stitch for 8 rows.

ROW 24 K1, K2tog, knit until three stitches remain, K2tog, K1. *You now have* 28 stitches.

ROW 25 Purl to end of row.

ROWS 26–37 Repeat Rows 24 and 25 six times. *You now have* 16 stitches.

ROW 38 K1, K2tog, knit until three stitches remain, K2tog, K1. *You now have* 14 stitches.

ROW 39 P1, P2tog, purl until three stitches remain, P2tog, P1. *You now have* 12 stitches.

ROWS 40 AND 41 Repeat Rows 38 and 39. *You now have* 8 stitches.

ROW 42 Repeat Row 38. *You now have* 6 stitches.

ROW 43 P1, P2tog twice, P1. *You now have* 4 stitches.

ROWS 44–46 Work in stockinette stitch for 3 rows.

ROW 47 P2tog twice. *You now have* 2 stitches.

ROW 48 AND 49 Work in stockinette stitch for 2 rows.

ROW 50 K2tog. Break yarn; thread back through last stitch. Pull to tighten. Weave in all ends.

I-Cord Stamen

SET UP Find the place between the flower and the stem where you stopped making the I-cord and started turning your work. A row below this spot, pick up any two consecutive green stitches on the inside (purl side) of the stem I-cord.

Using CE, * K2; without turning work, slide stitches across needle, then pull the yarn from the end of row and repeat from *. Repeat 30 times.

NEXT ROW   K2tog. Break yarn. Thread through last stitch and pull tight. Weave in end.

PREPARING TO FELT THE FLOWER

Weave in all ends. Orient the flower so the stamen side is facing you, and fold the outside edges of the petals inward at the stem until they overlap, as a real calla lily does. Tack 2" (5 cm) or so above the stem to hold the overlap in place. The stitches will disappear during felting.

FELTING

1 Follow My Basic Felting Technique on page 16. If you want the flower to felt longer than the purse, hold the purse above the water and dip the calla portion in as the water agitates.

2 When the purse is felted to your satisfaction, lay a towel on a flat surface, such as an ironing board, and place the purse on top. Arrange the purse as you would like it to dry: Make the corners square, make the top flap's edges even with the purse's corners, adjust the flower as you would like, then pin in place to make sure the purse stays exactly like this as it dries. Let dry completely before removing your pins.

3 Use a yarn needle and black yarn to tack the calla lily down to the front flap.

4 Now take your little black purse out for a night on the town!

WHAT'S AN I-CORD?

An I-cord is a round hollow tube that is knit on double-point needles. When thick, I-cords make sturdy straps for bags (see Petals & Stems Purse, page 57). When thin they make piping for edges, as on this clutch. I also use them as stems for flowers (see Elegant Lily, page 127). Make an I-cord by casting on the desired number of stitches onto a double-point needle. Without turning the work, slide the stitches across the needle. Pull yarn tightly from end of row behind the needle and knit the stitches. The first stitch you knit will be the first stitch you cast on. Slide the stitches before working each row.

Petals & Stems Purse

Many larger felted purses end up slouchy and sacklike unless they have stiff reinforcement, such as a board base or a metal frame. The heavy fabric just doesn't have the necessary structure on its own to make it stand up. But what knitter wants to sew in reinforcing material after all that knitting? The challenge is to knit some structure into the purse. The knit-in lining and vertical tucks along the sides and corners of this bag force it to stand tall and square. The tailored shape is further emphasized during the blocking process.

FINISHED MEASUREMENTS

Approximately 10" (25.5 cm) wide and 8" (20 cm) tall, with 5" (12.5 cm) gussets

YARN

Ella Rae Classic, 100% wool, 220 yds (201 m)/3.5 oz (100 g)

MC   Orange 27, 3 balls
CC   Cactus 26, 2 balls

NEEDLES

US #10 (6 mm) straight needles
US #8 (5 mm) or smaller straight needle
Set of US #10 (6 mm) double-point needles, to work the I-cord
One US #10 (6 mm) circular needle, 24" (60 cm) long, to work the lining

GAUGE

Any worsted-weight wool should yield the correct proportions, no matter your tension.

OTHER SUPPLIES

Yarn needle
Split-ring stitch markers

PLAN OF ACTION

This bag is knit from side to side, rather than from bottom to top as is often done. When the six body panels are completed, you pick up stitches along the edge of two panels, knit the base, then seam the other three sides of the base to the other panels before felting. You then use your circulars to pick up stitches along the top of the bag and knit in the lining. The entire bag is knit in stockinette stitch (knit one row, purl one row).

Panel 1

SET UP   Using MC and US #10 (6 mm) needles, cast on 50 stitches.

ROWS 1–32   Beginning at the bottom right, follow Panel 1 of the Petals & Stems Chart on page 61. *Note:* Unless otherwise noted, on odd-numbered rows you knit every stitch and follow the chart from right to left; on even-numbered rows you purl every stitch and follow the chart from left to right. Cross yarns each time you change colors to prevent holes. See Fair Isle and Felting on page 45.

NOTE   Mark Row 32 with a split-ring stitch marker. Over the next few rows, you create a small "tuck," which creates a ridge on the right side of the work. (See Tuck It In! on page 72.)

ROW 33 (RIGHT SIDE)   In MC only, purl through the back loop to the end to create a turning ridge.

ROW 34   Purl to the end of the row.

SET UP   With the smaller-size needle on the wrong side, pick up one stitch for each stitch in Row 32 (marked row). There is no need to introduce a new yarn when you do this; simply pull up the existing loops. See Picking Up Stitches Demystified, page 51. When you are picking up the stitches, be sure to work from right to left so that the point of the smaller-size needle ends up next to the point of the larger needle. You are going to join these picked-up stitches with the stitches on the larger needle to form the tuck.

ROW 35   Hold the needles parallel in your left hand with the right side of the piece facing you. Fold the work between the small and large needles on itself so the right side is visible and the wrong side is hidden inside of the tuck. The smaller-size needle will be in the back. With the free US #10 (6 mm) needle and CC, knit together the first stitch from each needle. Continue in this manner to knit together one stitch from each needle, in the following color sequence: 8 CC (the first stitch has already been knit in CC) 2 MC, 13 CC, 2 MC, 13 CC, 2 MC, 9 CC (50 stitches in all).

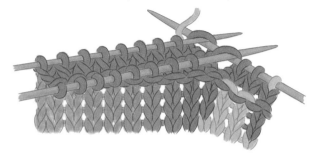

Panel 2

ROWS 36–66   Follow Panel 2 of the Petals & Stems Chart on page 61, noticing that Row 35 has already been knit. Place a split-ring marker on Row 66.

ROW 67 (RIGHT SIDE)   Using CC only, purl through the back loop to the end to create a turning ridge.

ROW 68   Purl to end of row.

SET UP   With a smaller-size needle on the wrong side, pick up one stitch for each stitch in Row 66 (marked row) to make the tuck.

ROW 69 (Row 1 on chart) Hold both needles parallel in your left hand with right sides facing you, then knit together one stitch from each needle as you did on Row 35, following this color sequence: 9 MC, 2 CC, 13 MC, 2 CC, 13 MC, 2 CC, 9 MC.

Remaining Panels

Repeat Rows 1–68 (Panels 1 and 2) twice more. (*Remember:* Each time you complete Panel 2, you have already knit Row 1 of the chart.) You will have 6 panels altogether. For Panel 6, knit the tuck using CC only, binding off as you proceed.

With right sides facing and using CC yarn and yarn needle, match the bound-off and cast-on edges and sew them together.

Turn the bag so the tucks are vertical. The completed bag will have two front panels, two back panels, and two side panels.

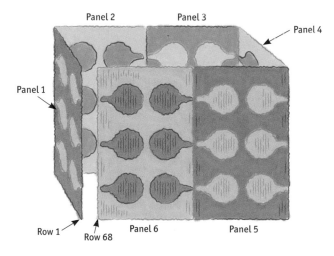

Panel 2 Panel 3 Panel 4

Panel 1

Panel 6 Panel 5

Row 1 Row 68

KNITTING THE BAG BASE

SET UP Decide which two panels you'd like to be the front of the bag. With a new strand of CC doubled, pick up and knit 52 stitches evenly spaced across the two front panels (26 stitches per panel). This is the bottom edge. When you pick up the stitches, skip the tuck stitches on the corners.

ROWS 1–26 Work in stockinette stitch.

Bind off.

Match the bound-off edge of the base to the bottom edge of the two back panels, and sew the edges together (right sides facing).

Seam the two side panels to the base. The tucks should stick out at the corners, making a 90-degree angle where the side panels meet the back and the front. When you stitch, try to accentuate this shaping. When you felt, any visible seaming stitches will disappear, so the stitching doesn't have to be perfect.

KNITTING THE LINING

SET UP Using the circular needle and MC, pick up and knit 156 stitches evenly spaced across all six panels (26 stitches per panel). Place marker.

ROUNDS 1–55 Knit to end of round. Slip marker.

ROUND 56 *K2tog, K37; repeat from * to end of round. *You now have* 152 stitches.

ROUND 57, 59, AND 61 Knit to end of round.

ROUND 58 *K2tog, K36; repeat from * to end of round. *You now have* 148 stitches.

ROUND 60 *K2tog, K35; repeat from * to end of round. *You now have* 144 stitches.

ROUND 62 *K2tog, K34; repeat from * to end of round. *You now have* 140 stitches.

ROUNDS 63–66 Knit to end of round.

Bind off.

KNITTING THE I-CORD HANDLES

For information on knitting I-cords, see What's an I-Cord? on page 55.

SET UP Using the double-point needles, pick up 5 stitches at the top (the lining side) of any one of the four tucks forming the bag's corners.

ROW 1 Using same color yarn as the tuck, knit to end of row.

ROW 2 Without turning work, slide stitches across needle. Pull yarn tightly from end of row behind needle and knit the 5 stitches.

ROWS 3–90 Repeat Row 2.

Bind off. Sew the end of the cord to the same color corner tuck two panels over. Repeat process on the opposite side, using the second color.

FELTING AND FINISHING

1 Follow My Basic Felting Technique on page 16.

2 Roll the purse in a terry-cloth towel and squeeze until all the excess water is removed. You will be working with the purse while it is damp, so set up in a place that can tolerate a little dripping water.

3 Turn the purse inside out and fold the lining down so that it covers the wrong side of the purse. Manipulate both the purse and the lining by stretching and pulling the fabric until the lining fits snugly against the purse. (If the lining is too long, don't worry about that for now. You'll trim it later.)

4 Using yarn needle and MC yarn, tack the lining securely to the corner and center tucks. A couple of stitches per tuck is plenty. The felt is so thick, there is no need to pass the needle through all layers. Simply catch enough of the tuck that the stitches hold the lining in place.

5 Slide the purse onto a box large enough that the purse is taut when pulled over it. (I use the box of my daughter's Hungry Hippos board game.)

6 Sew the lining to the inside base of the bag at the seam where the base meets the edges. If the lining doesn't match up perfectly to this seam, trim the lining before sewing.

7 Remove the purse, turn it so right side is facing and return it to the blocking box. Let the purse dry completely before removing it from the box. It should stand up on its own and be perfectly square.

Petals & Stems Chart

Repeat grid two times more (6 panels altogether), starting at Row 2 (a purl row) of the grid.

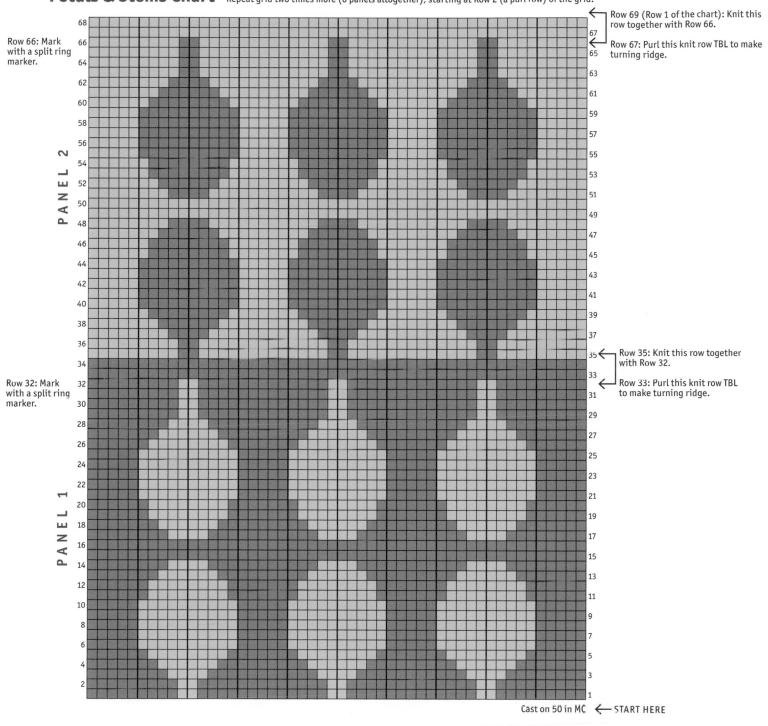

Row 69 (Row 1 of the chart): Knit this row together with Row 66.

Row 67: Purl this knit row TBL to make turning ridge.

Row 66: Mark with a split ring marker.

PANEL 2

Row 35: Knit this row together with Row 32.

Row 33: Purl this knit row TBL to make turning ridge.

Row 32: Mark with a split ring marker.

PANEL 1

Cast on 50 in MC ← START HERE

Checks & Spirals Backpack

Whimsical design elements bring this fun bag to life. Not only do the crochet chain spirals and Fair Isle check add visual interest, but they also make an otherwise simple project more entertaining to knit. The sturdy straps do double duty to carry *and* close the bag.

This bag is fail-safe. It's easy to knit and even if — oops — you leave it a little too long in the washer, it will maintain a sturdy, proportionate shape.

FINISHED MEASUREMENTS
15" (38 cm) high and 12" (30.5 cm) wide

YARN
Cascade 220, 100% wool, 220 yds (201 m)/3½ oz (100 g)

CA	Chocolate 2403, 2 skeins
CB	Summer Sky Heather 9452, 2 skeins
CC	Beige 8021, 1 skein
CD	Celery 9407, 1 skein

NEEDLES
One US #10 (6 mm) circular needle, 24" (60 cm) long
Smaller diameter circular needle, 24" (60 cm) long (optional, for three-needle bind off)
US #10 (6 mm) straight needles
A third US #10 (6 mm) or smaller straight needle

GAUGE
Any worsted-weight wool should yield the correct proportions, no matter your tension.

OTHER SUPPLIES
Split-ring stitch markers
Crochet hook, optional (for making spirals)
Yarn needle
Point protectors
Straight pins

PLAN OF ACTION
The backpack is knit in the round starting at its base and ending at its top. The pattern gives options to simplify more challenging areas: The Fair Isle strap can be modified to a quicker I-cord; the top channel can be secured using a simple overcast stitch or using a more complex three-needle bind off.

KNITTING THE BAG

SET UP Using the US #10 (6 mm) circular needle and CA, cast on 144 stitches. Join into a round, taking care not to twist the stitches. Place marker to show beginning of round.

ROUNDS 1–57 Knit to end of each round. Break off CA.

ROUNDS 58–96 Change to CB, and knit to end of each round. Break off CB.

Top Band

SET UP Place a split-ring stitch marker that will stay on the first stitch of Round 1 of the band. (Continue using the stitch marker that denotes the beginning of the rounds.) The band is knit in Fair Isle, so loosely carry colors not in use along the back. (See Fair Isle and Felting on page 45.) Begin knitting Fair Isle with CB, CC, and CD as follows:

ROUNDS 1–3 * K4 CC, K4 CD; repeat from * to end of round.

NOTE In the next round, you make the hole for the strap. Take care when carrying CD across the back that the yarn doesn't hang across the hole.

ROUND 4 Using CC, bind off 4 stitches. * K4 CD, K4 CC; repeat from * to end of round. (You will end with CD.)

ROUND 5 Using CC, cast on 4 stitches. * K4 CD, K4 CC; repeat from * to end of round. (You will end with CD.)

ROUND 6 Using CC, knit the newly cast-on stitches through back loop to tighten. * K4 CD, K4 CC; repeat from * to end of round. (You will end with CD.)

ROUND 7 * K4 CB, K4 CC; repeat from * to end of round.

ROUNDS 8–12 Repeat Round 7.

ROUNDS 13–18 Repeat Round 1.

ROUNDS 19–23 Repeat Round 7.

Channel for Strap

NOTE You are going to fold the checked band in half and attach it to the wrong side of the bag to create a hollow channel that will hold the I-cord drawstring/strap. If you wish, follow the procedure for Round 24 below, or refer to Three-Needle Bind-Off Method in the box on the facing page. I prefer the three-needle bind off because it creates a neater seam. You can pick your favorite method.

ROUND 24 Using CB, bind off.

Fold checked band in half with wrong sides facing each other. Starting at the marker that indicates the start of the band, seam the bound-off edge using CB and an overcast stitch to the first row in the check pattern on the wrong side.

KNITTING THE BOTTOM

SET UP With right side facing you and the work upside down, find the tail denoting the first cast-on stitch at the bottom of the bag. (This tail will be in CA.) Count 27 stitches to the left of the tail and mark this stitch. Including this stitch, using a US #10 (6 mm) straight needle, and working in the direction of the tail, pick up 55 stitches along the cast-on edge. Don't introduce a new yarn when you do this. (See Picking Up Stitches Demystified on page 51.) The tail should now be at the center of the needle. Leave marker.

ROW 1 Using CD, knit to end of row.

ROW 2 Purl to end of row.

ROWS 3–22 Repeat Rows 1 and 2. Put a point protector on the tip of the needle.

FINISHING THE BOTTOM

SET UP Orient work so the right side is facing you and the bag is upside down. The stitch marker you placed earlier is on the left. Including this marked stitch, count 17 stitches to the left along the cast-on edge of the bag. Beginning at the 18th stitch, use a US #10 (6 mm) or smaller straight needle to pick up 55 stitches along the cast-on edge. Do not introduce a new yarn.

THREE-NEEDLE BIND-OFF METHOD

1 Place point protectors on the tips of the circular needle that holds your work. Use a second 24" (60 cm) circular needle (use US #9 [5.5 mm] or smaller to make this easier) to pick up stitches as described below. Don't introduce a new yarn when you do this, simply pull up the loops and put them on your needle.

2 On the wrong side, beginning at the marker that indicates the start of the band, pick up one stitch for each stitch along the first row of the check pattern. You now have 144 stitches on the smaller needle.

3 Fold top band in half so its wrong sides are facing each other. The left-hand needles of each circular needle are parallel to each other.

4 Remove point protectors. Using the right-hand end of the larger circular needle, knit the first stitches on each needle together. Knit the second stitches on each needle together. Slip the first stitch over the second (as in the normal bind off). Continue knitting one stitch from each needle together and binding off in this way until all the stitches are bound off.

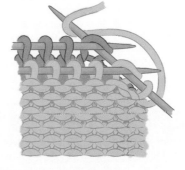

5 Break yarn, then draw the yarn through the last stitch and pull firmly to fasten off. Weave in any loose ends.

Turn the bag inside out so the wrong side is facing you. Remove the point protector from the US #10 (6 mm) needle holding the piece you knit for the bottom. Align both filled needles so their points face in the same direction. Using a third straight needle and CD, follow the Three-Needle Bind-Off Method (see page 65) to bind off all stitches from both needles.

Both sides of the bottom are open. Using CD, sew the openings closed from the wrong side. The stitching will disappear during felting. Weave in all loose ends.

KNITTING THE POCKET

SET UP   Using CD and US #10 (6 mm) straight needles, cast on 28 stitches.

ROW 1   Knit to end of row.

ROW 2   Purl to end of row.

ROWS 3–24   Repeat Rows 1 and 2.

BUTTONHOLE ROWS

ROW 25   *K6, bind off 2 stitches; repeat from * until 4 stitches remain; K4. *You now have* 22 stitches.

ROW 26   P5, cast on 2 stitches, * P6, cast on 2 stitches; repeat from * once; P5. *You now have* 28 stitches.

ROW 27   Knit to end of row, working the newly cast-on stitches through the back loop to tighten.

ROWS 28–30   Repeat Rows 1 and 2.

ROW 31   Bind off and weave in ends.

KNITTING THE CHECKED STRAP

NOTE   The straps are worked in Fair Isle using CB, CC, and CD. (See Fair Isle and Felting on page 45.)

SET UP   Using CC and US #10 (6 mm) straight needles, cast on 16 stitches.

ROW 1   * K4 CD, K4 CC; repeat from * to end of row.

ROW 2   * P4 CC, P4 CD; repeat from * to end of row.

ROWS 3–6   Repeat Rows 1 and 2.

ROW 7   * K4 CC, K4 CB; repeat from * to end of row.

ROW 8   * P4 CB, P4 CC; repeat from * to end of row.

ROWS 9–12   Repeat Rows 7 and 8.

ROWS 13–324   Repeat Rows 1–12. (You will have repeated the 12-row pattern 27 times.)

Using CC, bind off. Weave in any loose ends.

Fold strap in half lengthwise, wrong sides facing each other. Using a yarn needle and matching yarn, stitch the long edges together.

QUICK-VERSION STRAP

Done in Fair Isle, these straps take a long time to knit and seam. If you want the project to go more quickly, here are two options:

- Simply eliminate the checks and knit a solid-color strap using the same dimensions (16 stitches by 324 rows).
- Make a long, 10-stitch-wide I-cord. Work the cord for 324 rows. A cord will be thinner, but will still look great! (See What's an I-Cord? on page 55.)

FELTING

1 Weave in all loose ends.

2 Referring to My Basic Felting Technique on page 16), felt the three completed pieces before sewing them together. Check the strap regularly to see if it is tangling. If it is, pull it out of the water and disentangle: It will not felt evenly if it knots up.

3 When the pieces are felted to the desired size and consistency, remove them from your machine. You may want to felt some pieces longer than others, if necessary. Roll all pieces in a towel to get rid of excess water.

4 Finger-press all three pieces so that they are flat, and as square as possible. Dry completely before finishing.

FINISHING

Spirals

1 Using CA, crochet 7 chains 4.5" (11.25 cm) long. (For more information on crochet, see Spirals by Hand on page 68.)

2 Using CC, crochet 3 chains 4.5" (11.25 cm) long.

3 Arrange 3 CA chains and 3 CC chains in spirals on the felted pocket as shown. Pin. Using matching yarn, sew in place. You may want to put the pocket back into the washer for a minute or two so the spirals meld into the fabric. Pin and sew the remaining chains in spirals to the base of the bag. If the yarn seems too heavy to use for sewing, try splitting it in half along the ply.

pocket

base

Pocket

With matching yarn and yarn needle, pin and sew pocket directly below the bottom edge of the CB section on the center front of the bag. (The front is opposite the side with the hole for the I-cord strap.) Make the stitches as invisible as possible.

SPIRALS BY HAND

If you don't have a crochet hook handy, make the chains by hand. Make a slipknot at one end of a 2-foot (60 cm) length of yarn. * Reach through the loop and pull a portion of the yarn through; pull tight to make a second loop. Pull on the length of yarn to make the loop smaller. Repeat from * until the chain is 4½ " (11.25 cm) long.

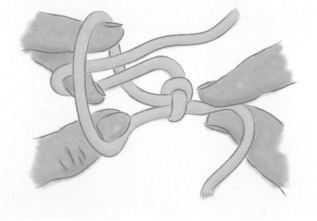

Bobbles

Using CB, crochet a chain about 3" (7.5 cm) long. Coil the chain onto itself so it looks like a tiny turban. Using matching yarn, stitch to hold piece together. Make two more. Sew one bobble directly behind each of the three holes of the pocket.

Strap

1 Thread the strap through the top channel, and pull all the way through. Continue until the bag is centered on the strap.

2 Check strap lengths by gathering the top closed, crossing straps at the hole, and pinning ends at the bottom right and left corners where CA and CD meet. Try on the bag and adjust the straps until you find the right fit.

3 Trim ends as necessary. Using matching yarn, invisibly sew the ends to the corners.

4 To help the new stitching disappear, you may wish to put the sewn-together backpack into the washer again, and let it felt for a minute or two more. Roll the bag in a towel, let dry, and enjoy wearing your new work of art out on the town!

Groovy Flower Purse

This purse carries its weight in versatility. The pattern includes options for short, handbag-style handles or a long, over-the-shoulder strap. The flower and gusset stripes create a retro '70s look, or skip the Fair Isle knitting altogether and enjoy a more sophisticated monochrome purse.

FINISHED MEASUREMENTS

Before felting: circle diameter = 9"
(23 cm)
After felting: circle diameter = 7"
(18 cm)

YARN

Cascade 220, 100% wool, 220 yds
(201 m)/3.5 oz (100 g)
CA   Flamingo Pink 7805, 2 skeins
CB   California Poppy 7826, 2 skeins

NEEDLES

One US #10 (6 mm) circular needle,
24" (60 cm) long
Any smaller diameter circular needle
(US #7 [4.5 mm] or less is ideal)
Set of US #10 (6 mm) double-point
needles

GAUGE

Any worsted-weight wool should yield
the correct proportions, no matter
your tension.

OTHER SUPPLIES

Yarn needle
Stitch marker
Large safety pin
Zipper for closure (Purchase the zipper
after you felt your purse. The final size
won't be exact until you've shrunk the
piece. Also, you can swap out the zipper for a snap, Velcro, or other closure
of your choice.)

PLAN OF ACTION

Groovy Flower Purse is knit in the
round in one piece so there is no
seaming at the finish. First you'll
knit the front disk and the Fair Isle
flower. Then you'll pick up stitches
to create the side gusset. You knit
the back last, repeating the flower
pattern. The key to success with
Groovy Flower Purse is to keep the
yarn slack at the back when working
the Fair Isle pattern.

KNITTING THE PURSE FRONT

SET UP Using US #10 (6 mm) circular needle and CA, cast on 100 stitches. Place marker to denote the beginning of the round. Join, being careful not to twist stitches.

ROUNDS 1–4 Knit to end of each round.

Short-handled style only

ROUND 5 Bind off 2 stitches, K26, bind off 2 stitches, knit to end of round.

ROUND 6 Cast on 2 stitches; K26, cast on 2 stitches, knit to end of round.

Long-handled style only

ROUND 5 Bind off 2 stitches; knit to end of round.

ROUND 6 Cast on 2 stitches; knit to end of round.

Both styles

ROUND 7 Knit to end of round. *Note:* When you reach each newly cast-on stitch, knit through back loop to tighten hole.

ROUNDS 8–9 Knit to end of each round.

ROUND 10 With smaller circular needle, pick up 1 stitch for each stitch along the cast-on edge of the work. *You now have* 100 stitches on both sets of circulars. (See Picking Up Stitches Demystified on page 51.) There's no need to introduce a new yarn as you pick up the stitches. You are going to join these picked-up stitches with the stitches on the larger needle to form a "tuck." (See Tuck It In!, below.)

ROUND 11 Fold the work between the small and large needles on itself so that wrong sides are facing each other and the tips of each left-hand needle are parallel. The smaller-size needle will be in the back. With the free larger needle in your right hand and the right side of the work facing you, knit the first stitch from each left-hand needle together. Continue in this manner to the end of the round. Break CA yarn.

TUCK IT IN!

I admit, the instructions for knitting in a tuck are quite complicated, but what is created in the end is really very simple: A tuck is just a hollow channel knit into your work.

If you were sewing, you'd make a tuck by folding your material back onto its wrong side and hemming it down. In knitting you do exactly the same thing except, instead of sewing the fabric down, you knit it down.

Tucks have several uses in felted items: They hold I-cord handles, they create structure, and they can provide texture and dimension that won't be lost when the piece is shrunk.

KNITTING THE FLOWER AND DISK

ROUND 1   Change to CB, and knit to end of round.

ROUND 2   * K2tog, K8; repeat from * to end of round. *You now have* 90 stitches.

ROUND 3   * K2tog, K16; repeat from * to end of round. *You now have* 85 stitches.

NOTE   Use both CA and CB for the next several rounds. Loosely carry the color not in use along the back of the work. (See Fair Isle and Felting on page 45.)

ROUND 4   K7 CB, K2 CA, * K15 CB, K2 CA; repeat from * to last 8 stitches, K8 CB.

ROUND 5   K6 CB, K4 CA, * K13 CB, K4 CA; repeat from * to last 7 stitches, K7 CB.

ROUND 6   K5 CB, K6 CA, * K11 CB, K6 CA; repeat from * to last 6 stitches, K6 CB.

ROUND 7   K4 CB, K8 CA, * K9 CB, K8 CA; repeat from * to last 5 stitches, K5 CB.

ROUND 8   K3 CB, K10 CA, * K7 CB, K10 CA; repeat from * to last 4 stitches, K4 CB.

ROUND 9   K2 CB, K12 CA, * K5 CB, K12 CA; repeat from * to last 3 stitches, K3 CB.

ROUND 10   K1 CB, K14 CA, * K3 CB, K14 CA; repeat from * to last 2 stitches, K2 CB.

ROUNDS 11–13   K16 CA, * K1 CB, K16 CA; repeat from * to last stitch, K1 CB.

ROUND 14   * Using CA, K7, K2tog, K7, then K1 CB; repeat from * to end of round. Break CB yarn. *You now have* 80 stitches.

ROUND 15   Using CA, * K2tog, K6; repeat from * to end of round. *You now have* 70 stitches.

ROUND 16   Knit.

ROUND 17   * K2tog, K5; repeat from * to end of round. *You now have* 60 stitches.

ROUND 18   Knit. Break CA yarn.

ROUND 19   Using CB, * K2tog, K4; repeat from * to end of round. *You now have* 50 stitches.

ROUND 20   Knit.

ROUND 21   * K2tog, K3; repeat from * to end of round. *You now have* 40 stitches.

ROUND 22   Knit.

ROUND 23   * K2tog, K2; repeat from * to end of round. *You now have* 30 stitches.

ROUND 24   Knit.

ROUND 25   * K2tog, K1; repeat from * to end of round. *You now have* 20 stitches.

ROUND 26 Knit.

ROUND 27 K2tog to end of round. *You now have* 10 stitches.

Break yarn, leaving a long tail. Thread tail back through remaining stitches. Pull tight (like a purse string), and on the wrong side, securely sew the hole at top closed. Weave in end.

STRIPED GUSSET MIDSECTION AND ZIPPER OPENING

SET UP Find the tail denoting the first cast-on stitch. With wrong side facing you and using US #10 (6 mm) circular needle, begin at this stitch to pick up 1 stitch for each cast-on stitch (100 stitches). *Note:* You've already folded and knit down the original cast-on edge when you formed the tuck. Because you knit 2 stitches together, each loop you are picking up is doubled. However, pull up only 1 loop per stitch, not both of them.

ROUND 1 Place marker. Orient work so right side is facing. * K2 CA, K2 CB; repeat from * to end of round. Slip marker on every round.

ROUNDS 2–5 Maintaining established color pattern, knit to end of each round.

NOTE Maintain established color pattern throughout this section, including the bind offs and cast ons.

ROUND 6 Knit 74, bind off 24 stitches. Knit to end of round. *You now have* 76 stitches.

ROUND 7 Knit 74. Cast on 24 stitches. Knit to end of round. *You now have* 100 stitches.

ROUND 8 Knit to end of round, tightening the newly cast-on stitches by knitting through the back loop.

ROUNDS 9–13 Knit to end of each round. Break CB yarn at end of Round 13.

KNITTING THE PURSE BACK

ROUNDS 1–4 Using CA, knit to end of round.

Short-handled style only

ROUND 5 Knit 70. Bind off 2 stitches, K26, bind off 2 stitches.

ROUND 6 Knit 70. Cast on 2 stitches, K26, cast on 2 stitches.

Long-handled style only

ROUND 5 Knit 70, bind off 2 stitches, knit to end of round.

ROUND 6 Knit to bound-off stitches, cast on 2 stitches, knit to end of round.

Both styles

ROUND 7 Knit to end of round. *Note:* When you reach each newly cast-on stitch, knit through back loop to tighten hole.

ROUNDS 8–10 Knit to end of round.

ROUND 11 Go to the round where you changed to CA (Round 1). Using the smaller circular needle and working on the wrong side, pick up 1 stitch for each stitch: 100 stitches in all. Fold the work between the small and large needles on itself so that wrong sides are facing each other and the tips of each left-hand needle are parallel. With the free larger needle in your right hand and the right side of the work facing you, knit the first stitch from each left-hand needle together. Continue in this manner to the end of the round.

Repeat Rounds 1–27 of Knitting the Flower and Disk (the purse front).

KNITTING THE I-CORDS

Short-handled style only

SET UP Using two double-point needles and CA, cast on 6 stitches. (See What's an I-Cord? on page 55.)

ROW 1 Knit to end of row.

ROW 2 Without turning work, slide stitches across needle. Pull yarn tightly from end of row behind needle and knit to end of row.

ROWS 3–203 Repeat Row 2. Depending on your tension, you will have about 1 yard. Bind off and weave in end. Make a second I-cord identical to the first.

Long-handled style only

SET UP Using CA and two double-point needles, cast on 6 stitches.

ROW 1 Knit one row.

ROW 2 Without turning work, slide stitches across needle. Pull the yarn tightly from the end of the row behind the needle and knit to the end of the row.

ROWS 3–353 Repeat Row 2. Depending on your tension, you will have about 2 yards. Bind off and weave in end.

FINISHING

NOTE This purse is finished in a slightly unusual style: You thread your I-cords through the edge channels before felting. This gives the purse stability and helps it maintain its shape. Refer to the illustrations on page 76 to place the cords; short handles and long handles are placed differently.

Short-handled style only

Attach a large safety pin to the end of the first I-cord. Using the pin as leverage, thread the I-cord through one of the two holes in the front circular ridge. Pull the cord all the way through the channel. Make sure the cord enters and exits the same hole. Holding on to the safety-pin end of the cord, stretch the purse's circular ridge to remove any puckering. Using a yarn needle and matching yarn, sew the end of the I-cord onto the original length of I-cord where it enters the hole. The long piece of I-cord left over will be your purse's handle. Sew its end at the second hole with yarn and yarn needle. Stitch all the way around the base of both holes so the I-cord is secure and the holes are sealed. Repeat this process with the second I-cord.

Long-handled style only

Attach a large safety pin to the end of the I-cord. Using the safety pin as leverage, thread the I-cord through the hole in the front circular ridge. Pull the cord all the way through the channel. Holding onto the I-cord, stretch the purse's circular ridge to remove any puckering. Sew the I-cord onto itself. Take the safety-pin end of the I-cord again and thread it through the hole on the back side. Pull the cord all the way through, remove puckering, and sew cord onto itself. Stitch all the way around the base of both holes so the I-cord is secure and the holes are sealed.

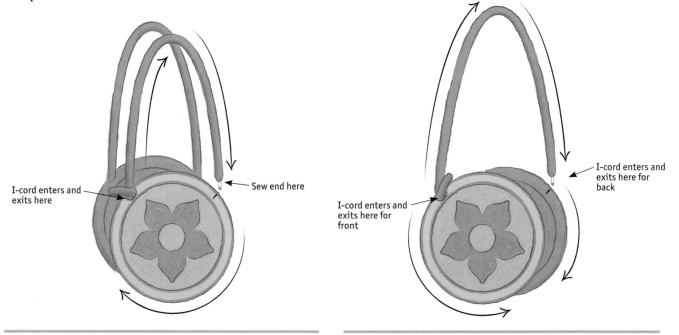

I-cord enters and exits here

Sew end here

I-cord enters and exits here for front

I-cord enters and exits here for back

FELTING

Follow My Basic Felting Technique on page 16. Be sure to check the felting regularly. If the straps tangle, untangle them or they will become misshapen. If the flower patterning puckers in the later stages of felting, turn the bag inside out and cut the carried yarns. Stretch aggressively to flatten.

INSTALLING THE ZIPPER (OPTIONAL)

1 Purchase a standard-size zipper that is as close as possible in size to the gusset opening. If necessary, you can cut the opening to fit the zipper.

2 Open zipper. With the purse right-side out, pin zipper so its head is up against one corner of the gusset opening and the top stop is at the other corner. Pin the fabric sides of the zipper along the inside of the gusset opening so that when closed, the zipper teeth are the only part of the zipper that is visible. Baste, if desired, so you can remove pins before sewing securely.

3 Using a matching sewing thread doubled, hand-sew along the backside from the top stop to the zipper head. Sew as close to the teeth as possible. Either a running stitch or a backstitch is okay, but a backstitch is stronger and will last longer. If you did not baste, remove pins as you progress. Repeat on the opposite side.

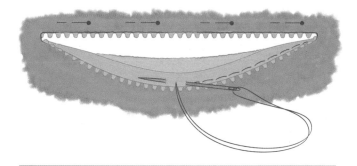

4 Turn the unsewn ends of the zipper at a downward angle and use double sewing thread to tack in place.

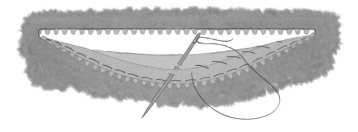

5 Use hemstitch to sew down the remaining zipper fabric.

Folded Brim Cloche

*S*hort-row shaping is the name of the game for this 1920s-inspired hat. Short rows let you mold your work without altering your stitch count. For this hat, that means you can form an arch along the brim's edge without starting at 150 stitches and decreasing to 90. For the flowers, that means you can extract 5 round petals out of an arrow-straight cast-on edge.

The hat is knit using a wool/silk/cashmere blend, so it felts soft, shiny, and not one bit fuzzy. If you've skipped felted hats for fear they'd be too heavy and scratchy, try the Folded Brim Cloche and lay your fears to rest. For an alternate flower that would also complement the style, try the Four-in-One Brooch on page 29.

SIZES AND FINISHED MEASUREMENTS

Size 1, Toddler 17"–18"
(43 cm–45.5 cm)
Size 2, Child 19"–20"
(48 cm–50.5 cm)
Size 3, Adult Medium 21"–22"
(53.5 cm–56 cm)
Size 4, Adult Large 23"–24"
(58.5–61 cm)

YARN

Jo Sharp Silkroad Aran, 85% wool/
10% silk/5% cashmere, 93 yds (85 m)/
1¾ oz (50 g)
MC   Opal 110, 2 balls
CC   Empire 137, 1 ball

NEEDLES

One US #10 (6 mm) circular needle,
16" (40 cm) long for sizes 1 and 2 or
24" (60 cm) long for sizes 3 and 4
Set of four US #10 (6 mm) double-
point needles

GAUGE

Before felting: 16 stitches = 4" (10 cm)
Use any worsted-weight 100% wool
or wool blend that felts and yields
a gauge similar to the gauge suggested when worked on US #10 (6mm)
needles.

OTHER SUPPLIES

Yarn needle
Split-ring stitch marker
Stitch marker

PLAN OF ACTION

The first step for success in knitting the cloche is selecting the correct size. If you have a small gauge and you are worried your hat will turn out too tiny, make the next largest size and felt it down. If your gauge is the same or large, make the size suggested. If you have a small gauge and want to make the largest-size hat, use a US #10.5 (6.5mm) needle. Remember you will have lots of room to get the sizing perfect when you felt.

	Size 1	Size 2	Size 3	Size 4

KNITTING THE BRIM

NOTE For the increases, knit into the front and back of a stitch to make two stitches. (See All Increases Are Not the Same on page 30.)

	Size 1	Size 2	Size 3	Size 4
SET UP Using the circular needle and MC, cast on	67 sts	76 sts	85 sts	95 sts

Place a marker to denote beginning of the round. Purl the first cast-on stitch to work in rounds. (You are purling the brim and knitting the hat, so that when you fold the brim up, the right side will be visible.)

	Size 1	Size 2	Size 3	Size 4
ROUND 1 Purl to end of round.				
ROUND 2 Inc 1, purl	22 sts	19 sts	17 sts	19 sts
Inc 1, purl to end of round. *You now have*	69 sts	78 sts	87 sts	97 sts
ROUND 3 Change to CC and purl	44 sts	38 sts	34 sts	38 sts
Inc 1, purl to end of round. *You now have*	70 sts	79 sts	88 sts	98 sts
Size 1 only Go to Shaping Brim with Short Rows.				
ROUND 4 Purl		57 sts	51 sts	57 sts
Inc 1, purl to end of round. *You now have*		80 sts	89 sts	99 sts
Size 2 only Go to Shaping Brim with Short Rows.				
ROUND 5 Purl			68 sts	76 sts
Inc 1, purl to end of round. *You now have*			90 sts	100 sts
ROUND 6 Purl to end of round.				
Size 3 only Go to Shaping Brim with Short Rows.				
ROUND 7 *(Size 4 only)* Purl to end of round.				

SHAPING BRIM WITH SHORT ROWS

SET UP   Now you are going to shape the arch in the brim using the short-row technique. A short row is made by turning your work at a specified point in the round and working a partial row, and then turning the work again and working a partial row, until the desired shape is achieved. Be sure to leave the round marker on the needle as you work the short rows.

ROW 1   Purl 12. Turn work.

ROW 2   Knit 14. Turn work.

ROW 3   Purl 16. Turn work.

ROW 4   Knit 18. Turn work.

ROW 5   Purl 20. Turn work.

ROW 6   Knit 22. Turn work.

ROW 7   Purl 24. Turn work.

ROW 8   Knit 26. Turn work.

ROW 9   Purl 28. Turn work.

ROW 10   Knit 30. Turn work.

ROW 11   Purl 32. Turn work.

ROW 12   Knit 34. Turn work.

ROW 13   Purl 36. Turn work.

FELTING = NO MORE SHORT-ROW HOLES

If you're new to short rows, you're in for a treat. This technique lets you quickly form single or multiple curves along an edge. Short rows are created by turning the piece before completing the row and working in the opposite direction. In standard knitting, it's important to avoid making a hole in your piece by maneuvering the yarn in a certain way at the start of each short row. In felting, however, there's no need to use this technique, because the holes disappear when the piece shrinks. If the holes bother you, close them when you weave in your ends.

ROW 14   Knit 38. Turn work.

ROW 15   Purl 40. Turn work.

ROW 16   Knit 42. Turn work.

ROW 17   Purl 44. Turn work.

ROW 18   Knit 46. Turn work.

ROW 19   Purl 48. Turn work.

ROW 20   Knit 50. Turn work.

(for Size 1, go now to Shaping the Hat and Crown.)

| | ROW 21 | Purl 52. Turn work. | | ROW 26 | Knit 62. Turn work. |

ROW 21 Purl 52. Turn work.

ROW 22 Knit 54. Turn work.

ROW 23 Purl 56. Turn work.

ROW 24 Knit 58. Turn work.

(for Size 2, go now to Shaping the Hat and Crown.)

ROW 25 Purl 60. Turn work.

ROW 26 Knit 62. Turn work.

ROW 27 Purl 64. Turn work.

ROW 28 Knit 66. Turn work.

(for Size 3, go now to Shaping the Hat and Crown.)

ROW 29 Purl 68. Turn work.

ROW 30 Knit 70. Turn work.

SHAPING THE HAT AND CROWN

	Size 1	Size 2	Size 3	Size 4
NEXT ROW Purl to the marker. You will now work in rounds for the rest of the hat.				
NOTE Change to double-point needles when the stitches get too tight on your circular needle.				
SET UP FOR ROUNDS Purl one round and break CC. You will knit the rest of the hat. The band will be in purl and the cap will be in knit.				
ROUND 1 Change to MC. Knit to end of round, increasing 5 stitches evenly across the round. *You now have*	75 sts	85 sts	95 sts	105 sts
ROUNDS 2–30 Knit to end of round.				

Size 1 only

ROUND 31 Knit, decreasing 5 stitches evenly across the round. *You now have* 70 stitches.

ROUND 32 * K2tog, K5; repeat from * to end of round. *You now have* 60 stitches.

ROUNDS 33, 35, 37, 39, 41   Knit to end of round.

ROUND 34   * K2tog, K4; repeat from * to end of round. *You now have* 50 stitches.

ROUND 36   * K2tog, K3; repeat from * to end of round. *You now have* 40 stitches.

ROUND 38   * K2tog, K2; repeat from * to end of round. *You now have* 30 stitches.

ROUND 40   * K2tog, K1; repeat from * to end of round. *You now have* 20 stitches.

ROUND 42   * K2tog to end of round. *You now have* 10 stitches.

Break yarn, leaving long tail. Thread tail through remaining stitches and pull tight (like a purse string). Sew the hole at the top using a yarn needle and the tail. Weave the remainder of the tail back into the work.

Size 2 only

ROUNDS 31–35   Knit to end of round.

ROUND 36   Knit to end of round, decreasing 5 stitches evenly across the round. *You now have* 80 stitches.

ROUND 37   * K2tog, K6; repeat from * to end of round. *You now have* 70 stitches.

ROUNDS 38, 40, 42, 44, 46, 48   Knit to end of round.

ROUND 39   * K2tog, K5; repeat from * to end of round. *You now have* 60 stitches.

ROUND 41   * K2tog, K4; repeat from * to end of round. *You now have* 50 stitches.

ROUND 43   * K2tog, K3; repeat from * to end of round. *You now have* 40 stitches.

ROUND 45   * K2tog, K2; repeat from * to end of round. *You now have* 30 stitches.

ROUND 47   * K2tog, K1; repeat from * to end of round. *You now have* 20 stitches.

ROUND 49   * K2tog to end of round. *You now have* 10 stitches.

Break yarn, leaving long tail. Thread tail through remaining stitches and pull tight (like a purse string). Sew the hole at the top using a yarn needle and the tail. Weave the remainder of the tail back into the work.

Size 3 only

ROUNDS 31–40   Knit to end of round.

ROUND 41   Knit to end of round, decreasing 5 stitches evenly across the round. *You now have* 90 stitches.

ROUND 42   * K2tog, K7; repeat from * to end of round. *You now have* 80 stitches.

ROUNDS 43, 45, 47, 49, 51, 53, AND 55   Knit to end of round.

ROUND 44   * K2tog, K6; repeat from * to end of round. *You now have* 70 stitches.

ROUND 46   * K2tog, K5; repeat from * to end of round. *You now have* 60 stitches.

ROUND 48   * K2tog, K4; repeat from * to end of round. *You now have* 50 stitches.

ROUND 50   * K2tog, K3; repeat from * to end of round. *You now have* 40 stitches.

ROUND 52   * K2tog, K2; repeat from * to end of round. *You now have* 30 stitches.

ROUND 54   * K2tog, K1; repeat from * to end of round. *You now have* 20 stitches.

ROUND 56   * K2tog to end of round. *You now have* 10 stitches.

Break yarn, leaving a long tail. Thread tail through remaining stitches and pull tight (like a purse string). Sew the hole at the top using a yarn needle and the tail. Weave the remainder of the tail back into the work.

Size 4 only
ROUNDS 31–45   Knit to end of round.

ROUND 46   Knit to end of round, decreasing 5 stitches evenly across the round. *You now have* 100 stitches.

ROUND 47   * K2tog, K8; repeat from * to end of round. *You now have* 90 stitches.

ROUNDS 48, 50, 52, 54, 56, 58, 60, AND 62   Knit to end of round.

ROUND 49   * K2tog, K7; repeat from * to end of round. *You now have* 80 stitches.

ROUND 51   * K2tog, K6; repeat from * to end of round. *You now have* 70 stitches.

ROUND 53   * K2tog, K5; repeat from * to end of round. *You now have* 60 stitches.

ROUND 55   * K2tog, K4; repeat from * to end of round. *You now have* 50 stitches.

ROUND 57   * K2tog, K3; repeat from * to end of round. *You now have* 40 stitches.

ROUND 59   * K2tog, K2; repeat from * to end of round. *You now have* 30 stitches.

ROUND 61   * K2tog, K1; repeat from * to end of round. *You now have* 20 stitches.

ROUND 63   * K2tog to end of round. *You now have* 10 stitches.

Break yarn, leaving a long tail. Thread tail through remaining stitches and pull tight (like a purse string). Sew the hole at the top using a yarn needle and the tail. Weave the remainder of the tail back into the work.

KNITTING THE FLOWER DECORATION

	Small Flower	Large Flower
NOTE Knit one small and one large flower, and then attach them to the hat by placing the smaller one over the larger and fastening them with a French knot. As with the brim on the Folded Brim Cloche, the petal shaping on this simple flower is achieved through short-row shaping.		
SET UP Using MC, cast on	30 sts	50 sts
ROW 1 Change to CC and knit	5 sts	8 sts
Short-Row Shaping		
SHORT ROW 1 Turn work and purl	3 sts	5 sts
SHORT ROW 2 Turn work and knit	4 sts	6 sts
SHORT ROW 3 Turn work and purl	5 sts	7 sts
SHORT ROW 4 Turn work and knit	10 sts	16 sts
SHORT ROWS 5–19 Repeat Short Rows 1–4, ending with a Short Row 3.		
SHORT ROW 20 Knit to end of row.		
Small Flower only		
ROW 2 * P1, P2tog; repeat from * to end of row. *You now have*	20 sts	
ROW 3 K2tog to end of row. *You now have*	10 sts	
ROW 4 P2tog to end of row. *You now have*	5 sts	

Large Flower only

ROW 2	* P3, P2tog; repeat from * to end of row.	40 sts
ROW 3	* K2tog, K2; repeat from * to end of row.	30 sts
ROW 4	* P1, P2tog; repeat from * to end of row.	20 sts
ROW 5	K2tog to end of row.	10 sts
ROW 6	P2tog to end of row.	5 sts

Both Sizes

Break yarn, leaving a long tail. Thread back through stitches on the needle. Remove stitches, and pull tail tight to close (like a purse string). Weave in all ends.

Seam flower along side edge to form a circle.

FELTING THE PIECES

1   Place the flowers in a mesh bag or pillowcase so you don't lose them in the washer. The hat can go directly into the basin. Felt the flowers and the hat at the same time, following My Basic Felting Technique on page 16. Because sizing is critical for hats, the optimum way to make sure the hat will fit is to try it on the head of the wearer as you are felting it. Trust me, I've had more than one wet hat on my head! And my kids have nightmares about me chasing them around the house with wet hats. Unfortunately for them, they are perfect Sizes 1 and 2!

2   Once you are satisfied with the size, block by sliding the hat onto a bowl that has the correct proportions. If you can't find a bowl, the hat will be fine as long as you dry it upright, so the dome of the hat is facing the ceiling. Make sure the dome is round and the brim is in exactly the position you like.

3   Sew small flower inside large flower using a French knot. (See Anatomy of a French Knot on page 33.) Sew flowers to side of hat.

After felting

Before felting

Tahoe Hat

Feminine styling breathes new life into this classic helmet-shaped hat. You'll work the earflaps first then form the brim and back of the hat by joining the flaps with cast-on stitches. Knitting the flowers on the smaller needles is a nice change after working with the worsted-weight yarn on the heavier needles.

SIZES AND FINISHED MEASUREMENTS

Size 1, Toddler 17"–18"
(43 cm–45.5 cm)
Size 2, Child 19"–20"
(48 cm–51 cm)
Size 3, Adult Medium 21"–22"
(53.5 cm–56 cm)
Size 4, Adult Large 23"–24"
(58.5 cm–61 cm)

YARN

Hat
Peruvian Collection Highland Wool,
100% wool, 109 yds (100 m)/1.75 oz
(50 g)
MC   Peridot 1477, 2 balls
CC   Victorian Violet 3741, 1 ball

NOTE   Divide CC into 4 balls
(2 for each earflap)

Flower Trim
Knit Picks Palette, 100% Peruvian
wool, fingering weight,
231 yds (211 m)/1.75 oz (50 g)
FWA   Nutmeg 23738, 1 ball
FWB   Hyacinth 23721, 1 ball
FWC   Tan 23736, 1 ball

NEEDLES

One US #10 (6 mm) circular needle,
16" (40 cm) long for sizes 1 and 2, or
24" (60 cm) long for sizes 3 and 4
Set of four US #10 (6 mm) double-
point needles
Set of four US #2 (2.75 mm) double-
point needles

GAUGE

20 stitches = 5½" (14 cm) in stockinette stitch, before felting and before
blocking. (See The Challenge of Hats
on page 19.)

OTHER SUPPLIES

Yarn needle
Stitch markers
Straight pins

PLAN OF ACTION

Use any worsted-weight 100% wool or wool blend that felts and yields a similar gauge when worked on US #10 (6 mm) needles. If your gauge is small, go up a size and felt the hat down. If your gauge is the same or large, make the size suggested. If you have a small gauge and want to make the largest hat, don't worry. The large hat is very big before felting. (It'll touch your shoulders when you put it on!) Even if you have a tiny gauge, you'll still have plenty of room to felt the hat down to the right size. If you are still nervous, go up to a US #10.5 needle (6.5 mm). Remember, no matter your gauge, the proportions will be correct and you can get the sizing perfect when you felt.

	Size 1	Size 2	Size 3	Size 4
NOTE If you prefer to make a cap without earflaps, use CC to cast on	70 sts	80 sts	90 sts	100 sts

Place marker and join, being careful not to twist stitches. Knit one round then change to MC and continue with Round 2 under Shaping the Hat and Crown on page 93.

KNITTING THE I-CORD

SET UP   Using the larger double-point needles and CC, cast on 2 stitches. (See What's an I-Cord? on page 55.)

ROW 1   Knit both stitches.

ROW 2   Without turning work, slide stitches across needle. Pull yarn tightly from end of row behind the needle and knit both stitches.

ROWS 3–42   Repeat Row 2.

SHAPING THE EARFLAP (MAKE 2)

NOTE   In this section, use your double-point needles as if they were regular straight needles and turn work after each row. For the increases, knit into the front and back of a stitch to make two stitches. (See All Increases Are Not the Same on page 30.) When you change to a new color, use a separate ball of yarn and do not break the old color. For advice on working with more than one yarn color, see Intarsia on page 143.

ROW 1   Using the 2 stitches on the needle, Inc 1 twice. *You now have 4 stitches.*

ROW 2   Purl to end of row.

	Size 1	Size 2	Size 3	Size 4
ROW 3 Inc 1, join MC, knit to last stitch, join second ball of CC, Inc 1. *You now have* 6 stitches (2 CC, 2 MC, 2 CC).				
ROW 4 Using CC, P2; using MC, purl to 2 stitches from the end; using CC, P2. Cross yarns each time you change colors to prevent holes.				
ROW 5 Using CC, Inc 1; using MC knit to the last stitch; using CC, Inc 1. *You now have*	8 sts	8 sts	8 sts	8 sts
ROW 6 Using CC, P2; using MC, purl to 2 stitches from the end; using CC, P2.				
ROWS 7–14 Repeat Rows 5 and 6, maintaining the colors as established. *You now have*	16 sts	16 sts	16 sts	16 sts
ROWS 15 AND 16 *(SIZES 2, 3, AND 4 ONLY)* Repeat Rows 5 and 6. *You now have*		18 sts	18 sts	18 sts
ROWS 17 AND 18 *(SIZES 3 AND 4 ONLY)* Repeat Rows 5 and 6. *You now have*			20 sts	20 sts
ROWS 19 AND 20 *(SIZE 4 ONLY)* Repeat Rows 5 and 6. *You now have*				22 sts
NEXT 2 ROWS *(ALL SIZES)* Staying in established color pattern, knit one row and purl the next.				
Don't break yarns. Place earflap on a circular needle for later use.				
Using new balls of MC and CC, make a second earflap in the same manner. When finished, leave second earflap on double-point needle and set aside for later use.				

	Size 1	Size 2	Size 3	Size 4

KNITTING THE HAT

NOTE You will begin by working with the earflap on the circular needle. Even though you are using a circular needle, you are going to work back and forth on it (as with a straight needle) for the first 5 rows.

	Size 1	Size 2	Size 3	Size 4
ROW 1 (RIGHT SIDE) Using CC, K2; using MC knit	12 sts	14 sts	16 sts	18 sts
Using CC, K2. Do not turn.				
Using CC, cast on	16 sts	18 sts	20 sts	22 sts

You will now join the second earflap that is on the double-point needle to the stitches you just cast on. Using the cast-on yarn, knit the first two stitches from the double-point needle onto the circular needle. Change to MC, knit the remaining MC stitches from the double-point needle onto the circulars. Change to CC, knit the last two stitches from the double-point needle onto the circulars.

	Size 1	Size 2	Size 3	Size 4
ROW 2 Turn work. Using CC, P2.				
Using MC, purl	12 sts	14 sts	16 sts	18 sts
Using CC, purl	20 sts	22 sts	24 sts	26 sts
Using MC, purl	12 sts	14 sts	16 sts	18 sts
Using CC, P2.				

Break CC yarns on inside edges of both earflaps. Weave in ends.

	Size 1	Size 2	Size 3	Size 4
ROW 3 Using CC, K2.				
Using MC, knit	44 sts	50 sts	56 sts	62 sts
Using CC, K2.				

	Size 1	Size 2	Size 3	Size 4
ROW 4 Using CC, P2.				
Using MC, purl	44 sts	50 sts	56 sts	62 sts
Using CC, P2.				
Turn work. Right side facing and still in CC, cast on	22 sts	26 sts	30 sts	34 sts
You now have	70 sts	80 sts	90 sts	100 sts

	Size 1	Size 2	Size 3	Size 4
ROW 5 Using CC, knit Break CC yarn. Using MC, knit to end.	24 sts	28 sts	32 sts	36 sts

SHAPING THE HAT AND CROWN

NOTE From here on, knit in rounds using MC. Place a marker to denote the beginning of the round.

ROUND 1 Using MC, join the CC stitches to the earflap.

Still using MC, knit to end of round. (You will work in only MC for the rest of the hat.) Break MC not in use and weave in end. Break CC; when you weave in the CC end, sew the gap closed between the CC stitches on the earflap and the brow brim.

ROUNDS 2–30 Knit to marker, slip marker on each round.

ROUNDS 31–35 (SIZES 2, 3, AND 4 ONLY) Knit to marker, slip marker on each round.

ROUNDS 36–40 (SIZES 3 AND 4 ONLY) Knit to marker, slip marker on each round.

NOTE Change to double-point needles when your stitches get too tight on your circular needle.

Size 1 only

ROUND 31 * K2tog, K5; repeat from * to end of round. *You now have* 60 stitches.

ROUNDS 32, 34, 36, 38, AND 40 Knit to end of round.

ROUND 33 * K2tog, K4; repeat from * to end of round. *You now have* 50 stitches.

ROUND 35 * K2tog, K3; repeat from * to end of round. *You now have* 40 stitches.

ROUND 37 * K2tog, K2; repeat from * to end of round. *You now have* 30 stitches.

ROUND 39 * K2tog, K1; repeat from * to end of round. *You now have* 20 stitches.

ROUND 41 K2tog to end of round. *You now have* 10 stitches.

Break yarn, leaving a long tail. Thread tail through remaining stitches and pull tight (like a purse string). Sew the hole at the top using a yarn needle and the tail. Weave the remainder of the tail back into the work.

Size 2 only

ROUND 36 * K2tog, K6; repeat from * to end of round. *You now have* 70 stitches.

ROUNDS 37, 39, 41, 43, 45, AND 47 Knit to end of round.

ROUND 38 * K2tog, K5; repeat from * to end of round. *You now have* 60 stitches.

ROUND 40 * K2tog, K4; repeat from * to end of round. *You now have* 50 stitches.

ROUND 42 * K2tog, K3; repeat from * to end of round. *You now have* 40 stitches.

ROUND 44 * K2tog, K2; repeat from * to end of round. *You now have* 30 stitches.

ROUND 46 * K2tog, K1; repeat from * to end of round. *You now have* 20 stitches.

ROUND 48 K2tog to end of round. *You now have* 10 stitches.

Break yarn, leaving a long tail. Thread tail through remaining stitches and pull tight (like a purse string). Sew the hole at the top using a yarn needle and the tail. Weave the remainder of the tail back into the work.

Size 3 only

ROUND 41 * K2tog, K7; repeat from * to end of row. *You now have* 80 stitches.

ROUNDS 42, 44, 46, 48, 50, 52, AND 54 Knit to end of round.

ROUND 43 * K2tog, K6; repeat from * to end of row. *You now have* 70 stitches.

ROUND 45 * K2tog, K5; repeat from * to end of row. *You now have* 60 stitches.

ROUND 47 * K2tog, K4; repeat from * to end of row. *You now have* 50 stitches.

ROUND 49 * K2tog, K3; repeat from * to end of row. *You now have* 40 stitches.

ROUND 51 * K2tog, K2; repeat from * to end of row. *You now have* 30 stitches.

ROUND 53 * K2tog, K1; repeat from * to end of row. *You now have* 20 stitches.

ROUND 55 K2tog until the end of the round. *You now have* 10 stitches.

Break yarn, leaving a long tail. Thread tail through remaining stitches and pull tight (like a purse string). Sew the hole at the top using a yarn needle and the tail. Weave the remainder of the tail back into the work.

Size 4 only

ROUND 41 * K2tog, K8; repeat from * to end of round. *You now have* 90 stitches.

ROUNDS 42, 44, 46, 48, 50, 52, 54, AND 56 Knit to end of round.

ROUND 43 * K2tog, K7; repeat from * to end of round. *You now have* 80 stitches.

ROUND 45 * K2tog, K6; repeat from * to end of round. *You now have* 70 stitches.

ROUND 47 * K2tog, K5; repeat from * to end of round. *You now have* 60 stitches.

ROUND 49 * K2tog, K4; repeat from * to end of round. *You now have* 50 stitches.

ROUND 51 * K2tog, K3; repeat from * to end of round. *You now have* 40 stitches.

ROUND 53 * K2tog, K2; repeat from * to end of round. *You now have* 30 stitches.

ROUND 55 * K2tog, K1; repeat from * to end of round. *You now have* 20 stitches.

ROUND 57 K2tog to end of round. *You now have* 10 stitches.

Break yarn, leaving a long tail. Thread tail through remaining stitches and pull tight (like a purse string). Sew the hole at the top using a yarn needle and the tail. Weave the remainder of the tail back into the work.

MAKING I-CORD TASSELS

SET UP Using the smaller double-point needle, pull up two stitches from the center top of the hat.

ROW 1 Using CC, knit both stitches.

ROW 2 Without turning work, slide stitches across needle. Pull yarn tightly from end of row behind needle and knit both stitches.

ROWS 3–18 Repeat Row 2.

Break yarn, leaving a small tail. Thread tail back through remaining stitches. Pull tight and weave in end.

Make 3 more tassels in the same manner (four tassels in all).

MAKING THE THREE-PETAL FLOWERS

BRIM FLOWERS For the brim, make three flowers in each of the fingering-weight yarns (3 FWA, 3 FWB, 3 FWC). Use two of the smaller double-point needles as straight needles, and work back and forth in rows.

First Petal

SET UP Using the smaller double-point needles, cast on 2 stitches. For the increases, knit into the front and back of a stitch to make two stitches. (See All Increases Are Not the Same on page 30.)

ROW 1 Inc 1 (knitwise) in each stitch. *You now have* 4 stitches.

ROW 2 Inc 1, P2, Inc 1. *You now have* 6 stitches.

ROW 3 Inc 1, K4, Inc 1. *You now have* 8 stitches.

ROW 4 Purl to end of row.

ROW 5 K2tog, K4, K2tog. *You now have* 6 stitches.

ROW 6 P2tog, P2, P2tog. *You now have* 4 stitches.

ROW 7 K2tog twice. *You now have* 2 stitches.

Bind off and weave in ends.

Second Petal

SET UP Using the smaller double-point needles, pull up the two stitches at the base of the petal (the two original cast-on stitches). Orient work so the knit side is facing you. Repeat Rows 1–7 as for First Petal, then bind off and weave in ends.

Third Petal

SET UP Pull up one loop from the base of each of the two completed petals. Orient work so the knit side is facing you. Repeat Rows 1–7 as for First Petal, then bind off and weave in ends.

I-CORD FLOWERS

Make 6 flowers to embellish the ends of the I-cords on the flaps and at the crown. Vary the colors of the flowers as desired.

SET UP Pull up two stitches from the end of the I-cord.

Follow the instructions for Making the Three-Petal Flowers on page 95.

FELTING

Place the brim flowers in a mesh bag or pillowcase, and tie closed. Felt the flowers in the bag, following My Basic Felting Technique on page 16. You can felt the hat at the same time, but do not place it in the bag. Since sizing is critical for hats, the best way to make sure the hat will fit is to try it on the head of the wearer as you are felting it. (See The Challenge of Hats, page 19.)

Once you are satisfied with the size, dry the hat upright, so the dome of the hat is facing the ceiling. Make sure the dome is rounded. If possible, find something to lift the hat so the earflaps can dry straight down. I use a small hat stand with a plastic bowl on top for this. Another option is to fill a flower pot with rocks, and poke a long knitting needle through the center. Balance a plastic bowl on the needle and slide the hat over the bowl.

FINISHING

Once the hat is dry, pin the flowers along the brim. Spread the petals out so they look like the photo on the facing page. Attach the flowers to the hat using French knots at each petal tip and in the center. (See Anatomy of a French Knot on page 33.)

Attach the brim flowers with French knots at the tips and centers.

Use French knots or small beads for the centers of the I-cord flowers.

Night Star Wrap

An elegant wrap that's felted? Felting is an unusual application for dainty evening wear, but once I made a swatch of Frog Tree's Chunky Alpaca and threw it in the washer, I knew the method would work. When shrunk, this alpaca fuzzes without matting, and it has enough weight to lend a nice drape to the wrap. For this project, I'm not looking for shrinkage, I'm looking for texture. The second the stitching gives way to the plush fuzziness of this yarn, I pull the wrap out of the washer. The luxurious softness of the alpaca coupled with the airy styling and bead embellishment will make this unlikely design a signature companion to your little black dress.

FINISHED MEASUREMENTS

11" (28 cm) wide and 41" (104 cm) long

NOTE Strangely, the finished size of this piece is very close before and after felting. When testing swatches, the width actually increased ½" in size, while the length shrunk by ½" on a 4" × 4" swatch. I account for this unusual felting in the pattern.

YARN

Frog Tree Chunky Alpaca, 100% alpaca, chunky weight, 54 yds (49 m)/1.75 oz (50 g)

CA   Black 100, 3 balls
CB   Grey 0012, 3 balls

NOTE Not all alpaca yarns felt without matting. Also, not all have the weight of Frog Tree's chunky version. I suggest using only Frog Tree Chunky Alpaca for this pattern.

NEEDLES

Two sets of US #10 (6 mm) straight needles, *or size you need to obtain correct gauge*

NOTE Using a circular needle may make it easier to slip the star parts on the needle in the correct direction.

GAUGE

Before felting: 4 stitches = 1" (2.5 cm)

OTHER SUPPLIES

Yarn needle
Hematite beads in a variety of shapes
Beading thread and needle
Yarn bobbins
Straight pins
Safety pin
Decorative clasp

PLAN OF ACTION

You knit the middle star first, beginning with four triangular arms and two rectangular joiners. As you work, you slide the arms and joiners onto the same long needle, then knit them together following a decrease pattern to form the star center. Next, you knit two half stars on the right side, then come back to the middle star and knit two half stars on the left side. As you knit each star, you connect it to its neighbor by picking up stitches from the joiners. The curve is created by the placement of the joiners: Some stars have five points, and some have six.

TIP   When you are done knitting the middle star, mark it with a safety pin so you can easily identify it as you work the rest of the pattern. For the increases, knit into the front and back of a stitch to make two stitches. (See All Increases Are Not the Same on page 30.)

Star Part 1: CA Arm

SET UP   Using CA, cast on 2 stitches.

ROW 1   Knit to end of row.

ROW 2   Purl to end of row.

ROW 3   Inc 1, knit to last stitch, Inc 1. *You now have 4 stitches.*

ROWS 4–6   Work in stockinette stitch (purl 1 row, knit 1 row).

ROW 7   Inc 1, knit to last stitch, Inc 1. *You now have 6 stitches.*

ROWS 8–19   Repeat Rows 4–7 three times. *You now have 12 stitches.*

ROW 20   Purl to end of row.

Measure a 7-foot (2.1 m) tail and break yarn. Use this tail to work the center of the star later. *Tip:* To keep yarn from tangling, wrap the tail onto a bobbin and pin it on the work while not in use.

Slide stitches onto another US #10 (6 mm) needle.

Star Part 2: CB Arm

Using CB, repeat Rows 1–20 of Star Part 1: CA Arm. Be sure to leave measured tail.

Slide stitches onto the needle with CA arm. Be sure that the knit sides of both are facing you. Wind long tail onto a bobbin.

WALKING ON THE WILD SIDE

As I said in the introduction, we'll break a few knitting rules several times throughout this book. In this pattern alone, there are three techniques that break knitting protocol:

● **Knot so wrong.** At finishing, you'll knot the seamed tips at the back. This is a big no-no in knitting but necessary for the wrap. If you skip it, the star tips will work their way apart in the washing machine and the whole item will come undone. I learned that the hard way.

● **Pulling up cast-on loops** — without introducing a new yarn, no less. This is disallowed because pulling up cast-on loops leaves large gaps and misshapes the work. If that's not bad enough, I then ask you to . . .

● **Knit the wrong way!** After you pull up the loops from the joiners, you knit in the opposite direction of the grain. Before you felt the wrap, the stars will resemble the worst knitted grafting job ever. Once it's felted though, no one will ever know! Now that's knitting on the edge.

Star Part 3: CA Joiner

SET UP   Using CA, cast on 12 stitches, leaving a 7-foot (2.1 m) tail coming from the first stitch you cast on. (You will use this yarn later.)

ROW 1   Knit to end of row.

ROW 2   Purl to end of row.

ROWS 3–14   Repeat Rows 1 and 2.

Measure a 7-foot (2.1 m) tail and break yarn. You now have long tails at the beginning and the end of the joiner. Slide stitches onto the needle next to the first two arms, knit-side facing you. Wind both long tails onto bobbins and pin on work to keep from tangling.

Star Parts 4–6

Make one more CB arm, one more CA arm, and one more CB joiner, and slide them on the needle holding the other arms and joiner. The right sides of all pieces should be facing in the same direction, and the arms and joiners should be arranged in the order shown below. *You now have* 72 stitches.

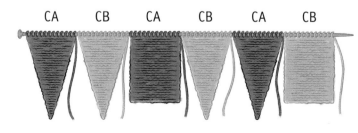

CA   CB   CA   CB   CA   CB

Star Center Decrease

NOTE   Using the long tails you measured out earlier, knit the following center decrease pattern as intarsia. As you work Row 1 below, join the star parts together by securely twisting the new yarn around the old on the wrong side. (See Intarsia, page 143.) The first time through the decrease pattern, you are working a 6-point star. The remaining stars will have 5 points and 3 points, so the number of stitches on your needle will change when you repeat this decrease pattern. Also, the color order will change as you move on to different stars. Use the color pattern established by the arms and joiners on your needle. The proper stitch counts for 5-point and 3-point stars are indicated below.

ROW 1   * Using CB, K5, K2tog, K5, change to CA, K5, K2tog, K5; repeat from * to end of row. *You now have* 66 stitches. (For 5-point stars: *You now have* 55 stitches. For 3-point stars: *You now have* 33 stitches.)

ROW 2   * Using CA, P5, P2tog, P4, change to CB, P5, P2tog, P4; repeat from * to the end of row. *You now have* 60 stitches. (For 5-point stars: *You now have* 50 stitches. For 3-point stars: *You now have* 30 stitches.)

ROW 3   * Using CB, K4, K2tog, K4, change to CA, K4, K2tog, K4; repeat from * to the end of row. *You now have* 54 stitches. (For 5-point stars: *You now have* 45 stitches. For 3-point stars: *You now have* 27 stitches.)

ROW 4 * Using CA, P4, P2tog, P3, change to CB, P4, P2tog, P3; repeat from * to the end of row. *You now have* 48 stitches. (For 5-point stars: *You now have* 40 stitches. For 3-point stars: *You now have* 24 stitches.)

ROW 5 * Using CB, K3, K2tog, K3, change to CA, K3, K2tog, K3; repeat from * to the end of row. *You now have* 42 stitches. (For 5-point stars: *You now have* 35 stitches. For 3-point stars: *You now have* 21 stitches.)

ROW 6 * Using CA, P3, P2tog, P2, change to CB, P3, P2tog, P2; repeat from * to the end of row. *You now have* 36 stitches. (For 5-point stars: *You now have* 30 stitches. For 3-point stars: *You now have* 18 stitches.)

ROW 7 * Using CB, K2, K2tog, K2, change to CA, K2, K2tog, K2; repeat from * to the end of row. *You now have* 30 stitches. (For 5-point stars: *You now have* 25 stitches. For 3-point stars: *You now have* 15 stitches.)

ROW 8 * Using CA, P2, P2tog, P1, change to CB, P2, P2tog, P1; repeat from * to the end of row. *You now have* 24 stitches. (For 5-point stars: *You now have* 20 stitches. For 3-point stars: *You now have* 12 stitches.)

ROW 9 * Using CB, K1, K2tog, K1, change to CA, K1, K2tog, K1; repeat from * to the end of row. *You now have* 18 stitches. (For 5-point stars: *You now have* 15 stitches. For 3-point stars: *You now have* 9 stitches.)

ROW 10 * Using CA, P1, P2tog, change to CB, P1, P2tog; repeat from * to the end of row. *You now have* 12 stitches. (For 5-point stars: *You now have* 10 stitches. For 3-point stars: *You now have* 6 stitches.)

ROW 11 * Using CB, K2tog, change to CA, K2tog; repeat from * to the end of row. *You now have* 6 stitches. (For 5-point stars: *You now have* 5 stitches. For 3-point stars: *You now have* 3 stitches.)

Weave tail from the last stitch back through the remaining stitches on your needle. Pull tight (like a purse string). Weave in that end. With the remaining center tails, pull tight and weave in so you can remove any gaps. Don't weave in the tails coming from the tips. You will use those later to sew the arms to each other.

For the 6-point and 5-point stars, seam the two edges together with matching yarn and yarn needle to form the circular center of the star. Stop seaming at the point where the arms break away from the center.

KNITTING STAR 2 (RIGHT OF MIDDLE STAR)

NOTE This is a 5-point star, connected to the middle star by a CA joiner.

1 Repeat Rows 1–20 of Knitting the Middle Star for the arms. Repeat Rows 1–14 for the joiner. Make 1 CB arm, 1 CB joiner, 1 CA arm, and 1 CB arm, arranging them on the needle in that order.

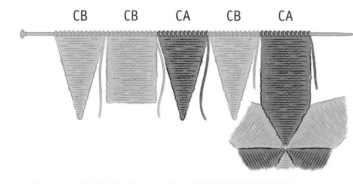

2 Lay the Middle Star on a flat surface, right side facing out. Arrange it so the CA joiner is on the right and the CB joiner is on the left.

3 Pick up the 12 cast-on stitches from the edge of the CA joiner on the Middle Star. *You now have* 60 stitches.

4 Starting with the CA joiner, repeat Rows 1–11 of the pattern for the Star Center Decrease, maintaining the correct color for each arm and joiner.

KNITTING STAR 3 (RIGHT OF STAR 2)

NOTE This is another 5-point star. It is connected to Star 2 by a CB joiner.

1 Repeating Rows 1–20 of Knitting the Middle Star for the arms and Rows 1–14 for the joiner, make 1 CA arm, 1 CB joiner, 1 CA arm, and 1 CB arm, arranging them on the needle in that order.

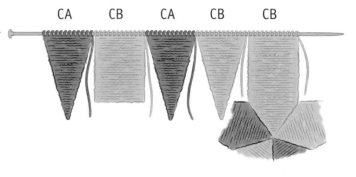

2 Pick up the 12 cast-on stitches from the edge of the CB joiner on Star 2. *You now have* 60 stitches.

3 Starting with the CB joiner, repeat Rows 1–11 of the pattern for the Star Center Decrease, maintaining the correct color for each arm and joiner.

KNITTING RIGHT HALF STAR

NOTE This is a 3-point half star. It is connected to Star 3 by a CB joiner.

1 Repeating Rows 1–20 of Knitting the Middle Star, make 2 CA arms.

Place one CA arm on your needle, pick up the 12 cast-on stitches from the edge of the CB joiner on Star 3, then place the second CA arm on the needle. *You now have* 36 stitches.

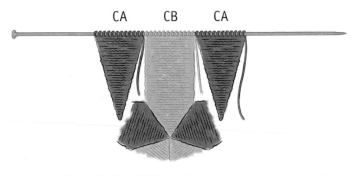

CA   CB   CA

2   Repeat Rows 1–11 of the pattern for the Star Center Decrease, maintaining the correct color for each arm and joiner.

KNITTING STAR 4 (LEFT OF MIDDLE STAR)

1   Return to the Middle Star to begin building the left side by adding onto the CB joiner of the Middle Star. This is a 5-point star.

2   Repeating Rows 1–20 of Knitting the Middle Star and Rows 1–14 of the joiner, make 1 CA arm, 1 CB arm, 1 CA joiner, and 1 CA arm. Arrange the pieces on your needle in that order.

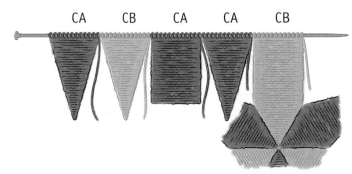

CA   CB   CA   CA   CB

3   Pick up the 12 cast-on stitches from the edge of the CB joiner of the Middle Star. *You now have* 60 stitches.

4   Starting with the CB joiner, repeat Rows 1–11 of the for the pattern Star Center Decrease, maintaining the correct color for each arm and joiner.

KNITTING STAR 5 (LEFT OF STAR 4)

NOTE   This is another 5-point star. It is connected to Star 4 by a CA joiner.

1   Repeating Rows 1–20 of Knitting the Middle Star and Rows 1–14 of the joiner, make 1 CA arm, 1 CB arm, 1 CA joiner, 1 CB arm. Arrange the pieces on your needle in that order. See illustration below.

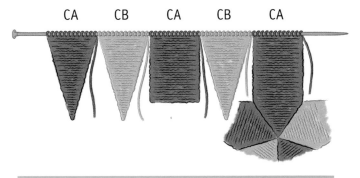

CA   CB   CA   CB   CA

2   Pick up the 12 cast-on stitches from the edge of the CA joiner of Star 4. *You now have* 60 stitches.

3   Starting with the CA joiner, repeat Rows 1–11 of the pattern for the Star Center Decrease, maintaining the correct color for each arm and joiner.

KNITTING LEFT HALF STAR

NOTE This is a 3-point half star. It is connected to Star 5 by a CA joiner.

1 Repeating Rows 1–20 of Knitting the Middle Star, make 2 CB arms.

2 Place the CB arm on your needle, pick up the 12 cast-on stitches from the edge of the CA joiner of Star 5, and put the CB arm on the needle. See illustration below. *You now have 36 stitches.*

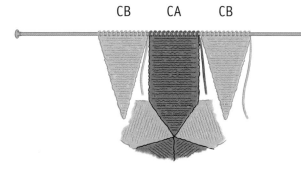

3 Repeat Rows 1–11 of the pattern for the Star Center Decrease, maintaining the correct color for each arm and joiner.

PUTTING THE PIECES TOGETHER

1 Lay the piece out on a flat surface, and orient it so the CA joining arm of the Middle Star is pointing to the right. Refer to the illustration below for where to join the arms. Pin to hold in place.

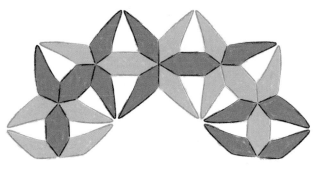

2 Thread the tails of each arm into a yarn needle and sew the arms together from tip to tip. Tie a secure knot on the wrong side before weaving the ends in. (It's okay to knot the yarn, because the knots will disappear during felting.)

FELTING AND FINISHING

Follow My Basic Felting Technique on page 16. This yarn takes only a couple of minutes to felt. Check it every minute to get the right texture, or you will shrink your piece. As soon as the fabric fluffs up cashmere-style, it is ready to pull out of the washer. Roll in a terry-cloth towel to remove excess water. Finger-press each star part so that they lay flat. Let dry completely before beading.

After the wrap is dry, use a beading needle and thread to sew beads to the center of each star and at each intersection between stars. Use a clasp of your choosing to close the wrap in front.

Tied Scarf

Try this project for a complete departure from standard knitting fare. The Tied Scarf's wavy silhouette is not achieved through knit-in shaping but from gathering and knotting the material *after* it's been worked and *before* it's been felted. When the scarf shrinks, the tied portions fuse into place. The fiber is a super-soft alpaca that does not fuzz or matt when felted. The resulting scarf is dramatic and extremely comfortable to wear.

FINISHED MEASUREMENTS
Before felting: 9' (274 cm) long and 7" (17.5 cm) wide
After felting: 5' (152 cm) long and 6" (15 cm) wide

YARN
Classic Elite Inca Print, 100% alpaca, 109 yds (100 m)/1¾ oz (50 g) Topiary 4648, 4 skeins

NEEDLES
US #10 (6 mm) straight needles

GAUGE
The gauge isn't critical. No matter your tension, the final size will be determined by what happens in the washing machine.

OTHER SUPPLIES
Split-ring stitch markers
Yarn needle

PLAN OF ACTION
The scarf's suggested prefelted length of 9 feet is merely a guideline. Adjust the scarf's length based on the height of the wearer — and on how ruffly you'd like it. If you like bunchy, dramatic ruffles, knit the scarf longer and scrunch aggressively in the tying process. If you'd like soft, undulating waves, knit the scarf shorter and keep the scrunching to a minimum.

KNITTING THE SCARF

SET UP   Cast on 30 stitches.

ROW 1   Knit, placing split-ring markers on the 10th and 20th stitches.

NEXT ROWS   Work in stockinette stitch until both ends of the scarf extend to the middle of the calf when the scarf is wrapped around the wearer's neck. As you work, place markers on the 10th and 20th stitches every 50th row, as well as the last knit row before binding off. Depending on the height of the wearer, the scarf will be about 9 feet (2.75 m), give or take a few inches.

Bind off and weave in all ends.

PLACING THE GATHERING STITCH

1   Thread a 20-foot (6 m) (longer if you make the scarf longer) strand of yarn through a yarn needle, matching ends so that the yarn is doubled.

2   Starting at the 10th stitch on the cast-on edge, run a continuous gathering stitch lengthwise along the scarf. Use the split-ring stitch markers as guides for your gathering stitches. When you reach the bind-off row, snip the yarn and remove the needle, leaving short tails; there will also be short tails on the cast-on edge.

3   Repeat the gathering stitch along the markers at the 20th stitches.

GATHERING AND TYING OFF

NOTE   The proportions will seem bizarre when the scarf is gathered and tied, but not yet felted.

1   Knot the tails of each row of gathering stitches at the cast-on edge. Make sure the knots are extremely secure so they won't come undone during felting. Weave the remaining tails back into the scarf.

2   Place the scarf on the wearer and position it so the tied-off end lands at the top of the thigh. Holding tightly to the gathering stitch tails on the other end of the scarf, push the scarf up to gather the material until it reaches the top of the thigh. Knot the tails on the bind-off edge to hold the gathers in place.

3   Lay the scarf on a flat surface. Trim the excess tails, and then sew them back into the scarf to secure the knots so that they do not come undone during felting.

4   Beginning at one end, push and pull the fabric until the gathers are evenly distributed. The gathers move somewhat during felting, giving the felted piece an interesting wavy effect.

FELTING THE SCARF

1 Follow My Basic Felting Technique on page 16. Set your washer to hot on a heavy-duty cycle with low water. Add the scarf after the water begins agitating. To check the felting progress, turn off the washer and pull a small section of the scarf out of the water. Have the stitches disappeared? Is the fabric noticeably stiff to the touch? Has the gathering string completely melded into the fabric so it is no longer possible to identify it? Does it look like the scarf in the photo on page 106? If so, your scarf is done. If you are unsure, it probably isn't done. Put it back in the water and felt it some more. The scrunching and knotting technique requires that the piece is felted *completely* in order for it to work. I suggest 9 feet, so the scarf has lots of room to shrink. Because it may take such a long time, however, it's important to babysit this scarf as you felt it to make sure it doesn't tangle in the wash.

2 When the scarf is felted to your satisfaction, wring it dry, then roll it in a towel and squeeze out any excess water. Accentuate the waves by shaping with your hands. I bunch the scarf accordion-style to dry, so that the waves are even further delineated.

WHERE DID THIS METHOD COME FROM?

The tying and knotting technique has its roots in Shibori, a Japanese form of tie-dyeing. In Shibori, fabric is manipulated by folding, crumpling, braiding, knotting, or twisting it before submerging it in dye. When the cloth is returned to its unmanipulated state, a pattern reveals itself in the spaces untouched by the dye. While most people look at Shibori strictly as a way to color textiles, several knitwear designers have seen its merit in a different arena — the three-dimensional shaping of fabric. For the Tied Scarf, I'm using a Shibori stitching technique to gather the fabric. The gather is then locked into place when the wool is felted. Other designers are tying marbles and other orblike objects into their knit wool. The result after felting: bulbous knitted bumps emerge from an otherwise flat sheet of felt. Cool!

Flower Petal Scarf

This scarf can be summed up in one word: fun. It's fun to knit, fun to felt, and fun to wear. The scarf is knit in one long piece; the only seaming occurs at the end when the tips of the petals are tacked together with a needle and yarn. Felting takes but a minute — allow just enough time to fluff the fabric up, cashmere-style. The fun continues with the array of color options. Select muted colors and the finished result is understated and airy. Select bold colors and watch the heads turn when you wear it around town.

FINISHED MEASUREMENTS

NOTE Strangely, the before and after felting measurements of this piece are very close. When testing swatches, the width actually *increased* ½" in size, while the length shrunk by ½" on a 4" × 4" swatch. I account for this unusual felting in the pattern.

62" (157 cm) long and 9" (24 cm) wide

YARN

Frog Tree Chunky Alpaca, 100% alpaca, chunky weight, 54 yds (49 m)/1¾ oz (50 g)

CA   Red 23, 3 balls
CB   Coral 213, 3 balls
CC   Wine 26, 3 balls

NOTE Not all alpaca yarns felt without matting, and not many have the weight of Frog Tree's chunky version. Be sure to make a swatch if you substitute another yarn for this one.

NEEDLES

Two pairs US #10 (6 mm) straight needles, *or size you need to obtain correct gauge*
A third needle (any size) or a stitch holder

GAUGE

Before felting: 4 stitches = 1" (2.5 cm)

OTHER SUPPLIES

Yarn needle
Yarn bobbin
Straight pins

PLAN OF ACTION

To create this scarf, you start on the left-hand side with the first flower, which includes five petals and one "joiner." As you complete the petals, you slide them onto another needle, and then join them following a decrease pattern that forms the flower's center. You then pick up stitches from the joiner and begin to build the next flower. You continue in this manner until you have knitted six flowers.

For the increases, knit into the front and back of a stitch to make two stitches. (See All Increases Are Not the Same on page 30.)

Petal 1

SET UP   Using CA, cast on 2 stitches.

ROWS 1 AND 2   Work stockinette stitch.

ROW 3   Inc 1, knit to last stitch, Inc 1. *You now have* 4 stitches.

ROWS 4–6   Work stockinette stitch.

ROW 7   Repeat Row 3. *You now have* 6 stitches.

ROWS 8–19   Repeat Rows 4–7. *You now have* 12 stitches.

ROW 20   Purl to end of row.

Measure a 7-foot (2.1 m) tail and break yarn. (You will use this tail to work the center of the flower later.) To keep yarn from tangling, wrap the tail into a bobbin and pin on work until it's time to use it again.

Slide stitches onto a spare needle, knit-side facing out.

Petal 2

SET UP   Using CC, repeat Rows 1–20 for Petal 1. Measure a 7-foot (2.1 m) tail, break the yarn, and slide stitches onto the same needle as Petal 1, knit-side facing out.

Petal 3

SET UP   Using CA, repeat Rows 1–20 for Petal 1. Measure the tail, break the yarn, and slide stitches onto the same needle as Petals 1 and 2, knit-side facing out.

Joiner

SET UP   Using CC, cast on 12 stitches, leaving a 7-foot (2.1 m) tail.

ROWS 1–14   Work in stockinette stitch.

Measure a 7-foot (2.1 m) tail and break yarn. Slide stitches onto the needle with the first three petals, knit-side facing out. Wind the beginning and ending tails onto bobbins and pin on work to keep from tangling.

Petals 4 and 5

Make two more petals, one using CA and one using CC. Slide these on the needle with the others, knit-sides facing. See illustration below for positioning.

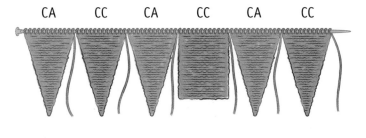

Middle of Flower Decrease Pattern

NOTE   You have 72 stitches on the needle total. You use the long tails you measured out earlier to work the center pattern as intarsia. (See Intarsia, page 143, for advice on this technique.) As you work your first row of the pattern below, join the petals together by securely twisting the yarn of the old color with the new color at the backside.

ROW 1   *Using CC, K5, K2tog, K5. Change to CA, K5, K2tog, K5; repeat from * to end of row. *You now have* 66 stitches.

ROW 2   *Using CA, P5, P2tog, P4. Change to CC. P5, P2tog, P4: repeat from * to end of row. *You now have* 60 stitches.

ROW 3   *Using CC, K4, K2tog, K4. Change to CA, K4, K2tog, K4; repeat from * to end of row. *You now have* 54 stitches.

ROW 4   *Using CA, P4, P2tog, P3. Change to CC. P4, P2tog, P3; repeat from * to end of row. *You now have* 48 stitches.

ROW 5   *Using CC, K3, K2tog, K3. Change to CA, K3, K2tog, K3; repeat from * to end of row. *You now have* 42 stitches.

ROW 6   *Using CA, P3, P2tog, P2. Change to CC. P3, P2tog, P2; repeat from * to end of row. *You now have* 36 stitches.

ROW 7   *Using CC, K2, K2tog, K2. Change to CA, K2, K2tog, K2; repeat from * to end of row. *You now have* 30 stitches.

ROW 8   *Using CA, P2, P2tog, P1. Change to CC. P2, P2tog, P1; repeat from * to end of row. *You now have* 24 stitches.

ROW 9   *Using CC, K1, K2tog, K1. Change to CA, K1, K2tog, K1; repeat from * to end of row. *You now have* 18 stitches.

ROW 10   *Using CA, P1, P2tog. Change to CC. P1, P2tog; repeat from * to end of row. *You now have* 12 stitches.

ROW 11   *Using CC, K2tog. Change to CA, K2tog; repeat from * to end of row. *You now have* 6 stitches.

Weave tail from the last stitch back through the remaining 6 stitches on your needle. Pull tight (like a purse string). Weave in that end. With the remaining center tails, pull tight and weave in so you can tighten and sew any gaps.

Seam the two sides together to form the center of the flower. Stop seaming at the point where the petals break away from the center. Weave in the center tails as you work every flower, but don't weave in the tails coming from the points. You will use those later to sew the petals to each other.

KNITTING THE SECOND FLOWER

NOTE   For this flower, you knit 2 CB petals, 2 CC petals, and 1 CB joiner.

SET UP Arrange the petals on your needle as in the illustration below. For the last petal on the needle (and the first you'll knit), pick up the 12 cast-on loops from First Flower's CC joiner.

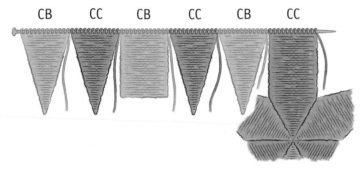

Repeat Rows 1–11 of the Middle of Flower Decrease Pattern, but maintain Second Flower's petal colors.

KNITTING THE THIRD FLOWER

NOTE For this flower, you knit 2 CA petals, 2 CB petals, and 1 CA joiner.

SET UP Arrange the petals on your needle as in the illustration below. For the last petal on the needle (and the first you'll knit), pick up the 12 cast-on loops from Second Flower's CB joiner.

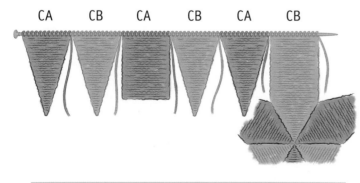

Repeat Rows 1–11 of the Middle of Flower Decrease Pattern but maintain Third Flower's petal colors.

KNITTING THE FOURTH FLOWER

NOTE For this flower, you knit 2 CC petals, 2 CA petals, and 1 CC joiner.

SET UP Arrange the petals on your needle as in the illustration below. For the last petal on the needle (and the first you'll knit), pick up the 12 cast-on loops from Third Flower's CA joiner.

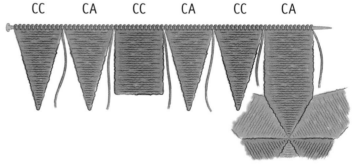

Repeat Rows 1–11 of the Middle of Flower Decrease Pattern but maintain Fourth Flower's petal colors.

KNITTING THE FIFTH FLOWER

NOTE For this flower, you knit 2 CB petals, 2 CC petals, and 1 CB joiner.

SET UP Arrange the petals on your needle as in the illustration below. For the last petal on the needle (and the first you'll knit), pick up the 12 cast-on loops from Fourth Flower's CC joiner.

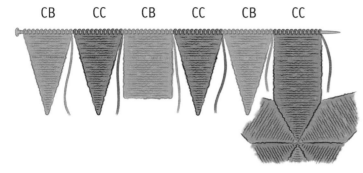

CB   CC   CB   CC   CB   CC

Repeat Rows 1–11 of the Middle of Flower Decrease Pattern but maintain Fifth Flower's petal colors.

KNITTING THE SIXTH (AND LAST!) FLOWER

NOTE For this flower, you knit 3 CA petals and 2 CB petals.

SET UP Arrange the petals on your needle as in the illustration below. For the last petal on the needle (and the first you'll knit), pick up the 12 cast-on loops from Fifth Flower's CB joiner.

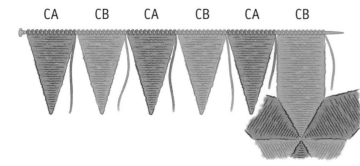

CA   CB   CA   CB   CA   CB

Repeat Rows 1–11 of the Middle of Flower Decrease Pattern but maintain Sixth Flower petal colors.

PUTTING THE PIECES TOGETHER

Refer to the illustration below to see where to join the flower petals.

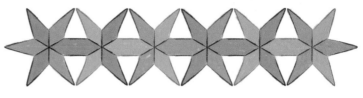

Using a yarn needle, sew the petals to each other. A good, secure way to do this is to thread the tails at the end of each petal and insert them into the point of the other petal, so that you can tie them in a close knot on the wrong side before weaving the ends in. It's okay to knot the yarn, because the knots will disappear during felting.

FELTING

Felt following My Basic Felting Technique on page 16.) Because of the yarn, the wrap takes only a couple of minutes to felt. It is finished when it appears fluffy and the stitches have disappeared.

FINISHING

Finger-press the petals flat and make all the flowers as even as possible. Leave flat and let dry completely before wearing. Snip any stray ends to clean up the surface.

Falling Leaf Pillow

This project is a prime example of the surprise nature of felting. Before the pillow is shrunk, it looks bad. It is misshapen, and the material puckers uncomfortably around the stitched-on leaves. But after a few magical minutes in your washing machine, you'll open the lid to find your ugly duckling morphed into a beautiful swan. The appliqué appears to be embossed upon the shiny wool/silk fabric and the pillow is perfectly proportioned. People will wonder how you made it, and you will marvel at its transformation.

FINISHED MEASUREMENTS
Before felting: 16" (41 cm) × 14" (35.5 cm)
After felting: 13½" (34 cm) × 11½" (29 cm)

YARN
Peruvian Collection Highland Silk, 80% Highland wool/20% silk, 122 yds (112 m)/1¾ oz (50 g)
MC Oxblood 2124, 3 balls
CC Celadon 2117, 1 ball (divided into 2 balls)

NEEDLES
US #10 (6 mm) straight needles

GAUGE
Any worsted-weight wool should yield the correct proportions, no matter your tension.

OTHER SUPPLIES
Yarn needle
Sewing needle
Matching sewing thread
100% polyester fiberfill, 2–4 oz (available at any craft or fabric store)
US H/8 (5 mm) crochet hook
Straight pins

PLAN OF ACTION
The pillow is knit in stockinette stitch with no shaping, making it a terrific project for newer knitters. While the pillow itself is as simple to knit as a scarf, knitting the leaves requires many quick increases and decreases. If you get off track (as you surely may when you're learning), just rip the row out. What's losing a row when it's only 5 stitches long?

KNITTING THE PILLOW FRONT

NOTE Be sure to wrap the new yarn around the old when changing colors across the rows.

SET UP Using CC, cast on 60 stitches.

ROW 1 Knit to end of row.

ROW 2 Purl to end of row

ROWS 3 AND 4 Repeat Rows 1 and 2 (stockinette stitch).

ROW 5 K4 CC, change to MC without breaking CC and K52 MC; change to second ball of CC without breaking MC and K4 CC.

ROW 6 P4 CC, P52 MC, P4 CC.

ROWS 7–84 Repeat Rows 5 and 6.

ROW 85 Change to CC and knit to end of row.

ROW 86 Purl to end of row.

ROWS 87 AND 88 Repeat Rows 1 and 2.

Bind off.

KNITTING THE PILLOW BACK

Repeat Rows 1–88 as for Knitting the Pillow Front.

KNITTING THE LEAVES

NOTE Make 4 large leaves, 2 medium leaves, and 3 small leaves. For the increases, knit into the front and back of a stitch to make two stitches. (See All Increases Are Not the Same on page 30.)

SET UP Using CC, cast on 1 stitch.

ROW 1 Knit.

ROW 2 Purl and Inc 1. *You now have* 2 stitches.

ROW 3 Inc 1, K1. *You now have* 3 stitches.

ROWS 4, 6, AND 8 Purl to end of row.

ROW 5 K1, Inc 1, K1. *You now have* 4 stitches.

ROW 7 K2, Inc 1, K1. *You now have* 5 stitches.

Small Leaf only

ROW 9 K2, K2tog, K1. *You now have* 4 stitches.

ROWS 10 AND 12 Purl to end of row.

ROW 11 K1, K2tog, K1. *You now have* 3 stitches.

ROW 13 K1, K2tog. *You now have* 2 stitches.

ROW 14 P2tog. *You now have* 1 stitch.

Break yarn and draw it back through last stitch. Pull tight, but do not weave in end.

Medium Leaf only

ROW 9 K2, Inc 1, K2. *You now have* 6 stitches.

ROW 10   Purl to end of row.

ROW 11   K2, K2tog, K2. *You now have* 5 stitches.

ROWS 12, 14, AND 16   Purl to end of row.

ROW 13   K2, K2tog, K1. *You now have* 4 stitches.

ROW 15   K1, K2tog, K1. *You now have* 3 stitches.

ROW 17   K1, K2tog. *You now have* 2 stitches.

ROW 18   P2tog. *You now have* 1 stitch.

Break yarn and thread back through last stitch. Pull tight, but don't weave in end.

Large Leaf only

ROW 9   K2, Inc 1, K2. *You now have* 6 stitches.

ROWS 10 AND 12   Purl to end of row.

ROW 11   K3, Inc 1, K2. *You now have* 7 stitches.

ROW 13   K3, K2tog, K2. *You now have* 6 stitches.

ROWS 14, 16, 18, AND 20   Purl.

ROW 15   K2, K2tog, K2. *You now have* 5 stitches.

ROW 17   K2, K2tog, K1. *You now have* 4 stitches.

ROW 19   K1, K2tog, K1. *You now have* 3 stitches.

ROW 21   K1, K2tog. *You now have* 2 stitches.

WHY THE ODD LEAF PLACEMENT?

After this pillow is shrunk, you will rotate it 90 degrees counterclockwise, and the leaf sprig will live in (the new) upper left-hand corner. It's hard to believe before you actually do it, but the bind-off edge ends up being longer than the side edge — a quirk of felting. This pillow is a great example of how knitted wool yarn shrinks considerably more lengthwise than widthwise. (See page 121.)

bind-off edge →

← cast-on edge

ROW 22 P2tog. *You now have* 1 stitch.

Break yarn and thread back through last stitch. Pull tight. Don't weave in end.

CROCHETING THE STEM

Crochet a 6" (15 cm) chain. If you don't have a crochet hook, you can make a chain by hand. (See Spirals by Hand on page 68.)

ATTACHING THE LEAF SPRIG

Arrange leaves and stem as shown on page 119. (See also page 121.) Pin in place. Take note of where the bind-off edge is in relation to the leaf sprig. The leaf placement will seem unusual, but when the pillow shrinks, everything will shift into proportion.

With a yarn needle and matching yarn, sew each leaflet in place, using an overstitch along the entire outline of the leaf. Remember that your stitches will disappear, so if, like me, you are not so great at appliqué, you won't be disappointed. Make sure all leaves are completely sewn down so that they uniformly meld into the fabric when it's felted, resulting in an embossed effect.

SEAMING THE PILLOW

Place the Front and Back of the pillow together with right sides facing each other, and use matching thread to seam along all four edges, leaving a 3" (7.5 cm) opening at the bottom right-hand corner.

FELTING THE PILLOW

Felt following My Basic Felting Technique on page 16. I tend to underfelt this pillow a bit so that it doesn't get too stiff. Pull the pillow out when the stitch definition has mostly disappeared and it is approximately the same size as the finished measurements above. Rinse by hand in cool water and squeeze out excess water by rolling in a terry-cloth towel.

FINISHING

1 Lay the pillow flat to dry, which can take up to two days — less if you place it in a warm room. Don't lay it in the sun, however, as the colors may fade. Make sure the pillow is completely dry before stuffing it.

2 Stuff your pillow with polyester fiberfill, then seam the opening closed, following these tips:

● Use a sewing needle and thread that matches the edging.

● Butt the seam edges against each other so the sewn seam will be flat. Keep the edges flush the whole time you sew.

BEFORE FELTING
Note placement of leaf sprig.

AFTER FELTING & FILLING

Funky Flower Pillow

No shaping and some very simple color changes make this project a great candidate for a beginning knitter. The pillow stands alone as an elegant silhouette, or it can be jazzed up with this trio of five-petal flowers, formed using short rows.

If you're a new knitter and find the color work daunting, skip it, and make three Simple Flowers instead.

FINISHED MEASUREMENTS
Before felting: 14" (35.5 cm) × 16" (41 cm)
After felting: 13½" (34 cm) × 11½" (29 cm)

YARN
Peruvian Collection Highland Silk, 80% Highland wool/20% silk, 122 yards (112 m)/1¾ oz (50 g)
MC Mesa Teal 1112, 3 balls
CC Celadon 2117, 1 ball (divided into 2 balls)

NEEDLES
US #10 (6 mm) straight needles

GAUGE
Any worsted-weight wool should yield the correct proportions, no matter your tension.

OTHER SUPPLIES
100% polyester fiberfill, 2–4 oz. (available at any craft or fabric store)
Yarn needle
Sewing needle
Matching thread
Straight pins

PLAN OF ACTION
The pillow is knit in two separate pieces in straight stockinette stitch. The pieces are seamed prior to felting. The short-row flowers are a fast and fun way for a beginner to learn the short-row technique.

KNITTING THE PILLOW FRONT

NOTE Be sure to wrap the new yarn around the old when changing colors across the rows.

SET UP Using CC, cast on 60 stitches.

ROW 1 Knit to end of row.

ROW 2 Purl to end of row

ROWS 3 AND 4 Repeat Rows 1 and 2 (stockinette stitch).

ROW 5 K4 CC, change to MC without breaking CC and K52 MC; change to second ball of CC without breaking MC and K4 CC.

ROW 6 P4 CC, P52 MC, P4 CC.

ROWS 7–84 Repeat Rows 5 and 6.

ROW 85 Change to CC and knit to end of row.

ROW 86 Purl to end of row.

ROWS 87 AND 88 Repeat Rows 1 and 2.

Bind off.

KNITTING THE PILLOW BACK

Repeat Rows 1–88 as for Knitting the Pillow Front.

KNITTING THE SIMPLE FLOWER

NOTE The petal shaping on this simple flower is achieved through short-row shaping. (See Felting = No More Short-Row Holes on page 81.)

SET UP Using CC, cast on 50 stitches.

SHORT ROWS K8, * turn, P5, turn, K6, turn, P7, turn, K16; repeat from * 4 more times. On the last repeat, end by knitting to the end of the row instead of K16.

ROW 1 * P3, P2tog; repeat from * to end of row. *You now have* 40 stitches.

ROW 2 * K2tog, K2; repeat from * to end of row. *You now have* 30 stitches.

ROW 3 * P1, P2tog; repeat from * to end of row. *You now have* 20 stitches.

ROW 4 K2tog to end of row. *You now have* 10 stitches.

Break yarn, leaving long tail, thread the yarn through a yarn needle, then draw the yarn back through stitches. Remove stitches from needle, and pull tail tight to close (like a purse string). Use the tail to seam flower along side edge to make center into a circle. Weave in all ends.

KNITTING THE STRIPED FLOWER

NOTE When knitting the two striped flowers, be sure to wrap the new yarn around the old when changing colors across the rows.

SET UP   Using MC, cast on 50 stitches.

Repeat Short Rows and Rows 1–4 for Knitting the Simple Flower, with this exception: Use CC for every knit stitch and MC for every purl stitch, even when you are working the short rows. Carry the color not in use across the back as you work.

Finish as for Knitting the Simple Flower.

KNITTING THE STRIPED PETAL FLOWER

SET UP   Using MC, cast on 50 stitches.

SHORT ROWS   Repeat Short Rows for Knitting the Simple Flower, with this exception: Work 2 stitches in MC, then work 2 stitches in CC. Continue alternating MC and CC, working all MC with MC and all CC with CC until you complete the short rows.

ROWS 1–4   Change to CC and repeat Rows 1–4 for Knitting the Simple Flower.

Finish as for Knitting the Simple Flower.

FINISHING THE FLOWERS

If desired, add French knots to the centers of the flowers. (See Anatomy of a French Knot on page 33.) You can pile them up or place one in the middle.

SEAMING THE PILLOW

Place the front and back of the pillow together with right sides facing each other, and use matching thread to seam along all four edges, leaving a 3" (7.5 cm) opening at any corner for filling.

FELTING THE PILLOW

1   Felt following My Basic Felting Technique on page 16. Place the flowers in a mesh laundry bag or a tied pillowcase so you don't lose them in the wash. Place the pillow directly in the basin. I tend to underfelt this pillow a bit so that it doesn't get too stiff. Pull the pillow out when the stitch definition has mostly disappeared and it is approximately the same size as the finished measurements listed on page 123.

2   Rinse by hand in cool water and squeeze out excess water by rolling in a terry-cloth towel.

3   Lay the pillow flat to dry, which can take up to two days — less if you place it in a warm room. Don't lay it in the sun, however, as the colors may fade. Make sure the pillow is completely dry before stuffing it.

4   Stuff your pillow with polyester fiberfill, then seam the opening closed. Follow the tips for Finishing on page 120.

SEWING ON THE FLOWERS

Arrange the flowers however you like: clustered to the side, three in a row, one in each corner, or in a diagonal line. Pin in place and attach the flower centers to the pillow using a yarn needle and matching yarn.

Elegant Lily

One of the most exciting aspects of felting is that it transforms a simple, knitted textile into a moldable material that has a sculptural quality. After shaping wet wool into dozens of hats, purses, and brooches, I discovered that felting didn't have to be limited to practical items. I realized it would be fun to shape the wool into just about anything I wanted. That's how Elegant Lily emerged.

FINISHED MEASUREMENTS
5"- (12.5 cm) long petals, 13" (33 cm) stems

YARN
Cascade 220, 100% wool, 220 yds (201 m)/3½ oz (100 g)

CA　　Natural 8010, 1 skein
CB　　Highland Green 9430, 1 skein

NOTE Not all whites felt. If you use a brand other than Cascade, please do a test swatch to make sure it felts.

NEEDLES
Set of four US #10 (6 mm) double-point needles

GAUGE
Any worsted-weight should yield the correct proportions, no matter your tension.

OTHER SUPPLIES
Stitch holder
Stitch marker
1 piece ¼" (6 mm) wide ribbon, 24" (61 cm) long
1 piece 18-gauge florist's wire, 24" (61 cm) long
1 piece 22-gauge cloth-wrapped florist's wire (for the stamen), 14" (36 cm)–21" (53 cm) long
Safety pins
Yellow beads (to top the stamen)
Needle-nose pliers
Yarn needle
Glue gun

PLAN OF ACTION
Elegant Lily is created in two sections: three large, outside petals on a long stem and a second group of inside petals with a funnel-shaped center. The two sections are knit and felted separately, and then they are joined at their centers to create the final flower. Florist's wire pulled through the I-cord stem keeps the lily standing tall.

KNITTING THE STEM

NOTE For the increases, knit into the front and back of a stitch to make two stitches. (See All Increases Are Not the Same on page 30.)

SET UP Using CB, cast on 4 stitches to start an I-cord. (See What's an I-Cord? on page 55.)

ROW 1 Knit to end of row.

ROW 2 Without turning work, slide stitches across needle. Pull the yarn tightly from the end of the row behind the needle and knit to end of row.

ROWS 3–70 Repeat Row 2.

ROWS 71–78 Knit to middle of row, Inc 1, knit to end of row. *You now have* 12 stitches.

KNITTING THE FLOWER BASE

SET UP Redistribute stitches evenly on 3 needles (4 stitches on each). Mark for beginning of round.

ROUNDS 1 AND 2 Using CA, knit to end of round.

ROUND 3 Increase 3 sts evenly across the round. *You now have* 15 stitches.

ROUND 4 Knit to end of round.

ROUNDS 5–8 Repeat Rounds 3 and 4. *You now have* 21 stitches.

ROUNDS 9–11 Knit to end of round.

KNITTING THE OUTER PETALS

SET UP Keep the first 7 stitches on needle and slide the remaining 14 stitches onto a holder.

NOTE From now on, use 2 double-point needles as straight needles, turning your work after every row. Work Row 1 with purlside facing you. Notice that you knit this row, even though purlside is facing.

Petal 1

ROW 1 Knit to end of row.

ROW 2 Purl to end of row.

ROWS 3, 5, AND 7 Increase 1, knit to last stitch, Inc 1. *You now have* 13 stitches.

ROWS 4, 6, AND 8 Purl to end of row.

ROW 9 Knit to end of row.

ROW 10 Purl to end of row.

ROWS 11–12 Repeat Rows 9 and 10.

ROW 13 K1, K2tog, knit to last 3 stitches, K2tog, K1. *You now have* 11 stitches.

ROW 14 Purl to end of row.

ROWS 15–20 Repeat Rows 13 and 14. *You now have* 5 stitches.

ROW 21 Knit to end of row.

ROW 22 Purl to end of row.

ROW 23 * K2tog, K1, K2tog. *You now have* 3 stitches.

ROW 24 Purl to end of row.

ROWS 25 AND 26 Repeat Rows 21 and 22.

ROW 27 K2tog, K1. *You now have* 2 stitches.

ROW 28 Purl to end of row.

ROW 29 K2tog. *You now have* 1 stitch. Leaving a tail, break yarn, and draw the tail back through the last stitch; pull tight. Weave in end.

Petal 2

SET UP Remove next 7 stitches from holder and place on a double-point needle. Orient work so purlside is facing.

Using a new strand of CA, repeat Rows 1–29 for Petal 1.

Petal 3

SET UP Remove last 7 stitches from holder and place on a double-point needle. Orient work so purlside is facing.

Using a new strand of CA, repeat Rows 1–29 for Petal 1.

Weave in all ends.

KNITTING THE INNER PETALS

SET UP Using CA, cast on 9 stitches. Distribute evenly over 3 double-point needles (three per needle). Join, being careful not to twist stitches.

ROUNDS 1–10 Knit to end of round.

Petal 1

SET UP Slide the first 3 stitches onto a double-point needle and place the remaining 6 stitches on a holder. Orient needle so purlside is facing. Notice that you *knit* the next row even though the purlside is facing.

ROW 1 Inc 1, K1, Inc 1. *You now have* 5 stitches.

ROW 2 Inc 1, P3, Inc 1. *You now have* 7 stitches.

ROWS 3–31 Repeat Rows 1–29 of Knitting the Outer Petals.

Petal 2

SET UP Remove next 3 stitches from the holder. Place on double-point needle. Orient work so purlside is facing.

Using a new strand of CA, repeat Rows 1–31 for Inner Petal 1.

Petal 3

SET UP Remove last 3 stitches from the holder. Place on double-point needle. Orient work so purlside is facing.

Using a new strand of CA, repeat rows 1–31 for Inner Petal 1.

FINISHING

Thread an approximately 24" (61 cm) length of ¼" (6 mm) ribbon through the center of the stem. Secure the ribbon to any petal and to the bottom of the stem using a safety pin on each side. *Note: Don't skip this important step. If you do, the I-cord will fuse to itself during felting, and you won't be able to get the florist's wire through.*

FELTING AND DRYING

Felt the two flower segments separately following My Basic Felting Technique on page 16. You may have to run the flower segments through more than one cycle before they're done. (But don't let them go through the spin cycle.) Your pieces are done if all the stitches have disappeared and the fabric is noticeably stiff to the touch. These pieces need to be shrunk *a lot!*

Remove pieces from washer and squeeze in a towel. Your petals will be floppy! Don't be sad about this — they'll perk up later.

Finger-press the petals to accentuate their tear-drop shape, and lay them out to dry completely before finishing.

FINISHING

Petals

1 Remove the pins and ribbon from the petals. Push the funnel-like portion of the second group of petals into the center of the first group. The more you push down, the more stability the petals will have. Using a yarn needle threaded with matching yarn, tack in place from the inside.

2 A garden lily's petals are arranged with the three lower-layer petals staggered perfectly between the three petals above them. Arrange your felted petals accordingly. Tack the petals to one another at their widest points.

Stem and Stamens

1 Using a pair of needle-nose pliers, make a ¼" (6 mm) eye-shaped hook at the top of the 24" (61 cm) florist's wire.

FIRST-AID FOR FORGETFULNESS

If you can't get the florist's wire through the I-cord stem because you forgot to put ribbon through it before felting, you'll have to make a new stem. Knit a new I-cord, put a ribbon through it, and felt it. Then, cut the top of the flower off the old I-cord and sew the flower to the new stem. Put the whole new flower in the washer, leaving the ribbon in the stem, and refelt until the fix-it stitches disappear.

2 For the stamens, cut four to six 3½" (9 cm) lengths of the 22-gauge cloth-wrapped florist's wire. Hook their bases to the hook on the large wire. Twist the smaller wires at the base of the hook to secure.

3 Push the large wire down through the I-cord channel, so that the cloth-wrapped stamens extend from the center of the petals. Pull the large wire from the bottom until the cloth-covered wires stand up straight.

4 Stitch the hook at the underside base of the flower so that it doesn't poke up through the flower.

5 Use a glue gun to attach the beads to the tips of the stamens.

6 At the bottom of the stem, trim the I-cord and/or the wire to the same length. Make an eye-shaped hook at the end of the wire. Using matching yarn, stitch around the eye to firmly attach.

7 Make a bunch and display in a bouquet!

STILL NOT ENOUGH SHAPE?

If your lily is too floppy, continue to felt it until it is very stiff, then hang it upside down to dry. When it is completely dry, tack the petals to each other with small stitches on the wrong side to add support and perkiness.

Stargazer Lily

Looking for more color?
Try our variation, the Stargazer Lily! Use 3 shades of red yarn along with the white (CA) and green (CB).

Stargazer Lily Chart

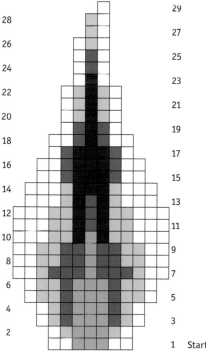

1   Start here, Knit row

Swirl Placemats

These circular placemats will lend such elegance to your dinner table, you won't want to put plates on them. The trick is to felt them long enough so that their centers lie flat. If the placemats still pop up slightly in the center, but the size and material feel right, you can solve the problem by drying the placemats with a heavy object on top. The piping edge ensures these placemats maintain a perfectly circular shape and that they won't pop up at the edges. They also need to be shrunk to the same size, so they match. This requires a lot of dipping in, pulling out, wringing out, and comparing. When dinner's over, remember to wash your placemats in cold water so they don't get any smaller!

YARN
Cascade 220, 100% wool, 220 yds
(201 m)/3½ oz (100 g)
CA   Lavender 7809, 1 skein
CB   Cream 8010, 1 skein
CC   Brown 2403, 1 skein

NEEDLES
US #10 (6 mm) straight needles
Or one US #10 (6mm) circular needle,
24" (60cm) long, worked as straight
needles. (The number of cast-on
stitches will be easier to handle on
circular needles.)
US #7 (4.5 mm) straight needles, or
smaller (to pick up stitches)

GAUGE
Any worsted-weight wool should yield
the correct proportions, no matter
your tension. The final size will be
determined during felting.

OTHER SUPPLIES
Yarn needle

PLAN OF ACTION
You create the placemat's circle shape
on straight needles by decreasing
at regular intervals throughout the
pattern. When the piece is done,
you seam it along the side edge to
complete the circle shape. Use a
cable cast on to start.

Small-Swirl Placemat

KNITTING THE PLACEMAT

SET UP Using CA and US #10 (6 mm) needles, cast on 154 stitches.

ROWS 1–10 Work in stockinette stitch (knit 1 row, purl 1 row). Break CA yarn and weave in end.

CREATING THE TUCK

ROW 11 Hold the piece with the wrong side facing you. With one of the smaller-size needles, pick up one stitch for each stitch along the cast-on edge. Do not work the stitches as you pick them up, and pick up from right to left so that the tip of the smaller-size needle ends up next to the tip of the US #10 (6 mm) needle. You are going to join these picked-up stitches with the stitches on the US #10 (6 mm) needle to form the tuck. Turn work so right side is facing you. Fold the work between the small and large needles on itself so that wrong sides are touching each other and the tips of the left-hand needles are parallel. (The smaller-size needle will be at the back.) Then, with the free US #10 (6 mm) needle and CC, knit together the first stitch on each needle (see illustration, page 58, and Tuck It In, page 72). Continue to knit together one stitch from each needle until you reach the end of the row.

ROW 12 Purl to end of row, decreasing 5 stitches evenly across the row. *You now have* 149 stitches.

ROW 13 Knit to end of row.

ROW 14 Purl and decrease 5 evenly across the row. *You now have* 144 stitches.

NOTE As you add the swirl, carry the colors not in use along the back.

ROW 15 Change to CA, K1; change to CC, K8; change to CB, K1; change to CC, knit to end of row.

ROW 16 Purl until you reach the CC stitch before CB; change to CB, P1; change to CC, P8; change to CA, P1; to CC, P1.

ROW 17 Staying in CC, K2; change to CA, K1; change to CC, K8; change to CB, K1; change to CC, knit to end of row.

ROW 18 Purl until you reach the CC stitch before CB; change to CB, P1; change to CC, P8; change to CA, P1; change to CC, P3.

ROW 19 (Swirls widen to 2 stitches.) Staying in CC, K4; change to CA, K2; change to CC, K7; change to CB, K2; change to CC, knit to end of row.

ROW 20 Purl until you reach one CC stitch before the CB stitches; change to CB, P2; change to CC, P7; change to CA, P2; change to CC, P5.

NOTE You have now established your color pattern: You are advancing the CC colors on your needles one stitch in the same direction for every row you work. Every fourth row you will add to the number of CA and CB stitches to make the swirls grow wider. As you decrease to form the placemat's circular shape, you will avoid the swirl pattern so

it is not disturbed. This is why the decreases are not always evenly spaced.

ROW 21 (First decrease row.) Using CC, K2tog. K4, change to CA, K2; change to CC, K7; change to CB, K2; change to CC, K7; *K2tog, K22; repeat from * to end of row. *You now have* 138 stitches.

ROW 22 Purl to one CC stitch before the CB stitches; change to CB, P2; change to CC, P7; change to CA, P2; change to CC, P6.

ROW 23 (Swirls widen to 3 stitches.) Using CC, K7; change to CA, K3; change to CC, K6; change to CB, K3; change to CC, knit to end of row.

ROW 24 Purl to one CC stitch before the CB stitches; change to CB, P3; change to CC, P6; change to CA, P3; change to CC, P8.

ROW 25 (Decrease row.) Using CC, K2tog, K7; change to CA, K3; change to CC, K6; change to CB, K3; change to CC, K2; *K2tog, K21; repeat from * to end of row. *You now have* 132 stitches.

ROW 26 Purl to one CC stitch before the CB stitches; change to CB, P3; change to CC, P6; change to CA, P3; change to CC, P9.

ROW 27 (Swirls widen to 4 stitches.) Using CC, K10; change to CA, K4; change to CC, K5; change to CB, K4; change to CC, knit to end of row.

ROW 28 Purl to one CC stitch before the CB stitches; change to CB, P4; change to CC, P5; change to CA, P4; change to CC, P11.

ROW 29 (Decrease row.) Using CC, K2tog, K10; change to CA, K4; change to CC, K5; change to CB, K4; change to CC, K2; * K2tog, K19; repeat from * to end of row. *You now have* 126 stitches.

ROW 30 Purl to one CC stitch before the CB stitches; change to CB, P4; change to CC, P5; change to CA, P4; change to CC, P12.

ROW 31 (Swirls widen to 5 stitches.) Using CC, K13; change to CA, K5; change to CC, K4; change to CB, K5; change to CC, knit to end of row.

ROW 32 Purl to one CC stitch before the CB stitches; change to CB, P5; change to CC, P4; change to CA, P5; change to CC, P14.

ROW 33 (Decrease row.) Using CC, K2tog, K10, K2tog, K1; change to CA, K5; change to CC, K4; change to CB, K5; change to CC, K13; * K2tog, K19; repeat from * to end of row. *You now have* 120 stitches.

ROW 34 Purl to one CC stitch before the CB stitches; change to CB, P5; change to CC, P4; change to CA, P5; change to CC, P14.

ROW 35 (Swirls widen to 6 stitches.) Using CC, K15; change to CA, K6; change to CC, K3; change to CB, K6; knit to end of row.

ROW 36 Purl to one CC stitch before the CB stitches; change to CB, P6; change to CC, P3; change to CA, P6; change to CC, P16.

ROW 37 (Decrease row.) Using CC, K2tog, K12, K2tog, K1; change to CA, K6; change to CC, K3; change to CB, K6; change to CC, K8; * K2tog, K18; repeat from * to end of row. *You now have* 114 stitches.

ROW 38 Purl to one CC stitch before the CB stitches; change to CB, P6; change to CC, P3; change to CA, P6; change to CC, P16.

ROW 39 (Swirls widen to 7 stitches.) Using CC, K17; change to CA, K7; change to CC, K2; change to CB, K7; change to CC, knit to end of row.

ROW 40 Purl to one CC stitch before the CB stitches; change to CB, P7; change to CC, P2; change to CA, P7; change to CC, P18.

ROW 41 (Decrease row.) Using CC, K2 tog, K14, K2tog, K1; change to CA, K7; change to CC, K2; change to CB, K7; change to CC, K3; * K2tog, K17; repeat from * to end of row. *You now have* 108 stitches.

ROW 42 Purl to one CC stitch before the CB stitches; change to CB, P7; change to CC, P2; change to CA, P7; change to CC, P18.

ROW 43 (Swirls widen to 8 stitches.) Using CC, K19; change to CA, K8; change to CC, K1; change to CB, K8; change to CC, knit to end of row.

ROW 44 Purl to one CC stitch before the CB stitches; change to CB, P8; change to CC, P1; change to CA, P8; change to CC, P20.

ROW 45 (Decrease row.) Using CC, K2tog, K16, K2tog, K1; change to CA, K8; change to CC, K1; change to CB, K8; change to CC, K2tog, K14; * K2tog, K16; repeat from * to end of row. *You now have* 102 stitches.

ROW 46 Purl to one CC stitch before the CB stitches; change to CB, P8; change to CC, P1; change to CA, P8; change to CC, P20.

ROW 47 (Swirls widen to 9 stitches.) Using CC, K21; change to CA, K9; change to CB, K9; change to CC, knit to end of row.

ROW 48 Purl in established color pattern. Be sure to carry the CC yarn behind the 18 swirl stitches.

ROW 49 (Decrease row.) Using CC, K2tog, K15, K2tog, K4; change to CA, K9; change to CB, K9; change to CC, K2tog, K8; * K2tog, K15; repeat from * to end of row. *You now have* 96 stitches.

ROW 50 Purl in established color pattern, advancing the swirl one stitch.

DECREASING WITHIN SWIRL PATTERN

SET UP You are now going to decrease 12 stitches per row every other row. In the previous decrease rows, you avoided the swirl pattern by making your decreases on either side of it. Now you will make decreases within the swirl pattern. Refer to the color charts at the bottom of this page and pages 138–39 for decrease rows. These show you how to treat the colors in the swirl. As you knit, don't forget to advance all colors one stitch in the correct direction. *Note:* The number of CA and CB stitches are not equal all the time.

Before knitting the next row, count the CC stitches you just purled. You should have 22 CC stitches, followed by 9 CA stitches and 9 CB stitches, and then the remaining 56 CC stitches. Read the accompanying charts from right to left. Only the swirl portion of each row is shown.

ROW 51 (Decrease row; see chart below.) * K2tog, K6; repeat from * to end of row. Work colors in swirl as indicated by the chart below. *You now have* 84 stitches.

For this chart, read from right to left. Only the swirl portion is shown.

Row 51

ROW 52   Purl in the established color pattern, advancing the swirl one stitch.

ROW 53   (Decrease row; see chart below.) * K2tog, K5; repeat from * to end of row. *You now have 72 stitches.*

ROW 54   Purl in the established color pattern, advancing the swirl one stitch.

ROW 55   (Decrease row; see chart below.) * K2tog, K4; repeat from * to end of row. *You now have 60 stitches.*

ROW 56   Purl in the established color pattern, advancing the swirl one stitch.

ROW 57   (Decrease row; see chart below.) * K2tog, K3; repeat from * to end of row. *You now have 48 stitches.*

ROW 58   Purl in the established color pattern, advancing the swirl one stitch.

ROW 59   (Decrease row; see chart below.) * K2tog, K2; repeat from * to end of row. *You now have 36 stitches.*

ROW 60   Purl in the established color pattern, advancing the swirl one stitch.

For all of the charts on this page and the next one, read from right to left. Only the swirl portion is shown.

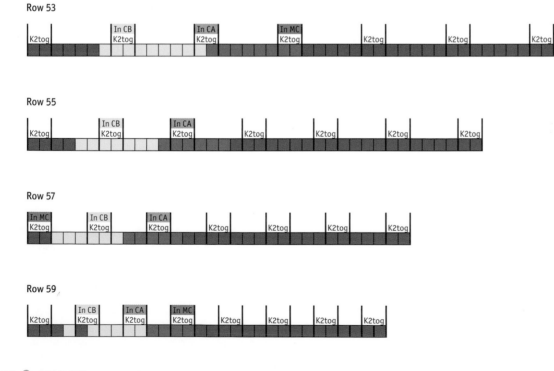

Row 53

Row 55

Row 57

Row 59

ROW 61 (Decrease row; see chart below.) * K2tog, K1; repeat from * to end of row. *You now have 24 stitches.*

ROW 62 Purl in the established color pattern, advancing the swirl one stitch.

ROW 63 (Last decrease row; see chart below.) K2tog to end of row. *You now have 12 stitches.*

Break all yarns, leaving long tail. Thread CC tail back through remaining stitches. Pull tight like a purse string. Weave in end.

FINISHING

Weave in all ends. With a yarn needle, seam the two edges together to form a circle, making sure to seam around both sides of the tuck.

FELTING

Follow My Basic Felting Technique on page 16.

Row 61

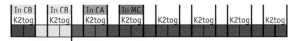

Row 63

Multi-Swirl Placemat

KNITTING THE PLACEMAT

SET UP Using CA and US #10 needles, cast on 154 stitches.

ROWS 1–10 Work in stockinette stitch (knit 1 row, purl 1 row). Break CA and weave in end.

CREATING THE TUCK

ROW 11 Hold the piece with the wrong side facing you. With one of the smaller-size needles, pick up one stitch for each stitch along the cast-on edge. Do not work the stitches as you pick them up, and pick up from right to left so that the tip of the smaller-size needle ends up next to the tip of the US #10 (6 mm) needle. You are going to join these picked-up stitches with the stitches on the US #10 (6 mm) needle to form the tuck. Turn work so right side is facing you. Fold the work between the small and large needles on itself so that wrong sides are touching each other and the tips of the left-hand needles are parallel. (The smaller-size needle will be at the back.) Then, with the free US #10 (6 mm) needle and CC, knit together the first stitch on each needle. (See illustration, page 58, and Tuck It In, page 72.) Continue to knit together one stitch from each needle until you reach the end of the row.

SETTING UP THE COLOR BANDS

ROW 12 Using CC, P4, P2tog, P19; change to CB, P8, P2tog, P16; change to CA, P13, P2tog, P11; change to second ball of CC, P17, P2tog, P7; change to second ball of CB, P21, P2tog, P3; change to second ball of CA, P25. *You now have 149 stitches.*

ROW 13 Using CA, K25; using CB, K25; using CC, K25; using CA, K25; using CB, K25; using CC, K24.

ROW 14 Using CC, P24; using CB, P3, P2tog, P20; using CA, P8, P2tog, P15; using CC, P12, P2tog, P11; using CB, P16, P2tog, P7; using CA, P20, P2tog, P3. *You now have 144 stitches.*

ROW 15 Using CA, K24; using CB, K24; using CC, K24; using CA, K24; using CB, K24; using CC, K24.

NOTE At this point, intarsia color bands begin to move diagonally.

ROW 16 Using CC, P23; using CB, P24; using CA, P24; using CC, P24; using CB, P24; using CA, P24; change to third ball of CC, P1 (seventh color band).

ROW 17 Using CC, K2; using CA, K24; using CB, K24; using CC, K24; using CA, K24; using CB, K24; using CC, K22.

ROW 18 Using CC, P21; using CB, P24; using CA, P24; using CC, P24; using CB, P24; using CA, P24; using CC, P3.

ROW 19 Using CC, K4; using CA, K24; using CB, K24; using CC, K24; using CA, K24; using CB, K24; using CC, K20.

ROW 20 Using CC, P19; using CB, P24; using CA, P24; using CC, P24; using CB, P24; using CA, P24; using CC, P5.

NOTE You have now established your color pattern: each color moves one stitch in the same direction every row. Continue in this established color pattern as you decrease. The decrease rows begin with the next row.

ROW 21 * K22, K2tog; repeat from * to end. *You now have 138 stitches.*

ROWS 22–24 Work in stockinette stitch in established color pattern.

ROW 25 * K21, K2tog; repeat from * to end. *You now have 132 stitches.*

ROWS 26–28 Work in stockinette stitch in established color pattern.

ROW 29 * K20, K2tog; repeat from * to end. *You now have 126 stitches.*

ROWS 30–32 Work in stockinette stitch in established color pattern.

ROW 33 * K19, K2tog; repeat from * to end. *You now have 120 stitches.*

ROW 34 Purl in established color pattern. This is the end of the CC diagonal band on the left; break this yarn. Each color band is 20 stitches wide.

ROW 35   Knit in established color pattern.

ROW 36   Purl in established color pattern until 1 stitch remains. Using third ball of CB, P1.

ROW 37   * K18, K2tog; repeat from * to end. *You now have* 114 stitches.

ROWS 38–40   Work in stockinette stitch in established color pattern.

ROW 41   * K17, K2tog; repeat from * to end. *You now have* 108 stitches.

ROWS 42–44   Work in stockinette stitch in established color pattern.

ROW 45   * K16, K2tog; repeat from * to end. *You now have* 102 stitches.

ROW 46–48   Work in stockinette stitch in established color pattern.

ROW 49   * K15, K2tog; repeat from * to end. *You now have* 96 stitches.

ROW 50   Purl in established color pattern. This is the end of the CB diagonal band on the left; break this yarn.

ROW 51   Knit in established color pattern.

ROW 52   Purl in established color pattern until 1 stitch remains. Using third ball of CA, P1.

NOTE   At this point, you begin decreasing every other row, 12 stitches per row. When you work the purl rows, don't forget to advance all colors one stitch in the correct direction.

ROW 53   * K6, K2tog; repeat from * to end. *You now have* 84 stitches.

ROW 54   Purl in established color pattern.

ROW 55   * K5, K2tog; repeat from * to end. *You now have* 72 stitches.

ROW 56   Purl in established color pattern.

ROW 57   * K4, K2tog; repeat from * to end. *You now have* 60 stitches.

ROW 58   Purl in established color pattern.

ROW 59   * K3, K2tog; repeat from * to end. *You now have* 48 stitches.

ROW 60   Purl in established color pattern. This is the end of the CA diagonal band on the left; break this yarn.

ROW 61   * K2, K2tog; repeat from * to end. *You now have* 36 stitches.

ROW 62   Purl in established color pattern until 1 stitch remains. Using CC, P1.

NOTE   On the next decrease row, you knit together stitches of two different colors.

ROW 63   Using CC, K1, K2tog; using CA, K1, K2tog, K1, K2tog; using CB, K1, K2tog, K1, K2tog; using CC, K1, K2tog, K1, K2tog; using CA, K1, K2tog, K1, K2tog; using CB, K1, K2tog, K1, K2tog; using CC, K1, K2tog. *You now have* 24 stitches.

ROW 64   Using CC, P2; using CB, P4; using CA, P4; using CC, P4; using CB, P4; using CA, P4; using CC, P2.

ROW 65   Using CC, K2tog, K2tog; using CA, K2tog, K2tog; using CB, K2tog, K2tog; using CC, K2tog, K2tog; using CA, K2tog, K2tog; using CB, K2tog, K2tog. *You now have* 12 stitches.

Break each length of yarn, leaving long tails. Thread CB tail back through remaining stitches. Pull tight (like a purse string). Weave in the end.

FINISHING

Weave in all ends. Seam the two edges together to form a cone, making sure to seam around both sides of the tuck.

FELTING

Follow My Basic Felting Technique on page 16. The placemat will lay flat when it is done. If it pops up, continue felting. If you feel the placemat is the right size, but it continues to pop up, place a heavy object on it and let it dry completely. The object will make the placemat take longer to dry, but it will also ensure the mat always lies flat.

INTARSIA

Intarsia is a method of working with large blocks of color. Rather than carrying the colors across the back of the work, as with Fair Isle, intarsia requires that you use separate yarns for each new color block. To keep the different yarns under control, roll each one into a small ball or wind it onto a yarn bobbin. As you end one color and begin another, you twist the new yarn around the old so holes won't form in the work.

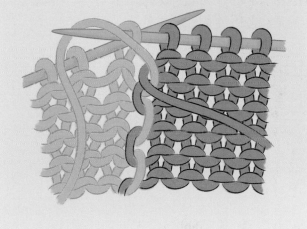

Bobble Napkin Rings

FINISHED MEASUREMENTS

7" (18 cm) long, including bobbles

YARN

Cascade 220, 100% wool, 220 yds
(201 m)/3½ oz (100 g)
CA   Lavender 7809, 20 yds (18 m)
CB   Cream 8010, 20 yds (18 m)
CC   Brown 2403, 20 yds (18 m)

NEEDLES

US #10 (6 mm) straight needles

GAUGE

Any worsted-weight yarn should yield
the corrrect proportions, no matter
your tension.

OTHER SUPPLIES

Yarn needle
Crochet hook, optional (for making
the loops)

KNITTING THE BOBBLES

Make 3, one in each color.

SET UP   Cast on 12 stitches, leaving a 10" (25 cm) tail.

ROW 1   Knit to end of row.

ROW 2   Purl to end of row.

ROW 3   K2tog to end of row. *You now have 6 stitches.*

ROW 4   P2tog to end of row. *You now have 3 stitches.*

Break yarn, leaving a 6" (15 cm) tail.

SHAPING THE BOBBLE

1   Thread tail through yarn needle, and draw the tail through the remaining stitches, taking them off the needle. Pull tight (like a purse string), then seam the two sides together to create a small cone. Still using the same threaded needle, pick up each stitch along the cast-on edge, then pull the tail through these stitches. Stuff cast-on tail into the center, then pull tight so the piece gathers into a little ball. Sew hole closed and weave in remaining end.

2   Using CA, crochet a 12" (30.5 cm) chain. Make it longer if you have extra-large napkins. (See Spirals by Hand on page 68.) Join the last chain to the first to form a continuous loop. Weave in the tails.

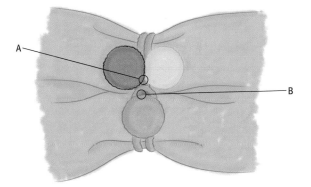

3   Sew two of the bobbles side by side, very close together, at the point where you joined the chain (A). Sew the third bobble at the halfway point (6" (15 cm) from the paired bobbles at B).

FELTING

Place napkin ring in a mesh bag before felting so you don't lose it in the machine. Felt following My Basic Felting Technique on page 16. Give these small items a long time to felt: The longer you felt them, the fluffier and rounder the bobbles will get.

USING THE NAPKIN RINGS

Lay the napkin ring on a flat surface, and place the folded napkin on top of it. Fold the two sides of the ring toward the middle of the napkin, and then connect them by tucking the side with the single bobble under the loop at the two bobbles. The tension created between the napkin and the pulling of bobbles holds the three bobbles together in a cluster.

Resources

I would like to thank the following yarn companies for providing the wonderful yarn for the projects in this book. I've included their Web sites so you can easily find and purchase the yarn. Most of these yarn manufacturers/distributors provide listings of retail outlets for their yarns, or the yarns are available for purchase directly from their Web site.

Jo Sharp Pty Ltd
P.O. Box 1018
Fremantle 6959
Australia
+61 8 9430 9699
www.josharp.com.au

Elann.com, Inc.
(for Peruvian Collection yarns)
CANADA:
P.O. Box 18125
1215C-56th Street
Delta BC V4L 2M4

UNITED STATES:
P.O. Box 1018
Point Roberts, WA 98281-1018
(604) 952-4096
www.elann.com

Cascade Yarns
P.O. Box 58168
Tukwila, WA 98138
(206) 574-0440
www.cascadeyarns.com

K. F. I.
(for patterns requiring Ella Rae Classic yarn)
P.O. Box 336
315 Bayview Avenue
Amityville, NY 11701
(516) 546-3600
www.knittingfever.com

Classic Elite Yarns
122 Western Avenue
Lowell, MA 01851-1434
(978) 453-2837
Fax: (978) 452-3085
www.classiceliteyarns.com

Knit Picks/Crafts Americana Group
13118 N.E. 4th Street
Vancouver, WA 98684
(800) 574-1323
www.knitpicks.com

Index

Page numbers in **bold** indicate charts and tables; page numbers in *italic* indicate an illustrations.

Other Storey Titles
You Will Enjoy

Knit One, Felt Two, by Kathleen Taylor.
Twenty-five spectacular projects to transform items knit large and loose into thick, cozy, felted garments and accessories.
176 pages. Paper. ISBN 1-58017-497-3.

Knit Scarves!, by Candi Jensen.
Fifteen patterns for colorful, cozy scarves, plus advice on needle choices and yarn alternatives.
96 pages. Die-cut paper-over-board. ISBN 1-58017-577-5.

Knit Socks!, by Betsy Lee McCarthy.
The latest addition to a best-selling series — fifteen patterns for all levels of knitters, paired with advice on knitting in the round on five needles.
144 pages. Die-cut paper-over-board. ISBN 1-58017-537-6.

The Knitting Answer Book, by Margaret Radcliffe.
Answers for every yarn crisis — an indispensable addition to every knitter's project bag.
400 pages. Flexibind with cloth spine. ISBN 1-58017-599-6.

Knitting Loves Crochet, by Candi Jensen.
A collection of designs where soft, shapely knitting meets pretty, crocheted edgings and flowers.
192 pages. Paper. ISBN 1-58017-842-1.

Knitting Rules!, by Stephanie Pearl-McPhee.
A sourcebook of invaluable advice, woven with witty insights and wry reflections in celebration of the knitting life.
224 pages. Paper. ISBN 1-58017-834-0.

One-Skein Wonders, edited by Judith Durant.
One hundred and one projects for all those single skeins in your stash.
240 pages. Paper. ISBN 1-58017-645-3.

These and other books from Storey Publishing are available
wherever quality books are sold or by calling 1-800-441-5700.
Visit us at *www.storey.com*.